EVERYDAY
BIBLE PROMISES
AND
DEVOTIONS

FOR MEN

EVERYDAY
BIBLE PROMISES
AND
DEVOTIONS

FOR MEN

BARBOUR BOOKS

An Imprint of Barbour Publishing, Inc.

© 2013 by Barbour Publishing, Inc.

Text previously appeared in *The KJV Daily Promise Bible* and *The Daily Bible Promise Book*, published by Barbour Publishing.

ISBN 978-1-64352-626-3

All scripture quotations are taken from the King James Version of the Bible.

Published by Barbour Books, an imprint of Barbour Publishing, Inc., 1810 Barbour Drive, Uhrichsville, Ohio 44683, www.barbourbooks.com

Our mission is to inspire the world with the life-changing message of the Bible.

Printed in China.

INTRODUCTION

Many people would like to read through the Bible in a year—but we know, from personal experience, that can be a real challenge. That's why we created *Everyday Bible Promises and Devotions for Men*—to give you the encouragement you need as you begin this life-changing journey.

In addition to daily scripture readings for every day of the year—an Old Testament, New Testament, and either Psalms or Proverbs passage—this book also features 365 challenging and encouraging devotional thoughts, each highlighting a particular Bible promise from that day's scripture selection.

Each day's reading should take 15 to 30 minutes to complete. If you stay with it, you'll soon be able to say, "I read through the Bible in a year!"—and you'll undoubtedly find your life changed by the great promises of God's Word.

The Publisher

DAY 1

GENESIS 1–2; MATTHEW 1; PSALM 1

*And the Lord God said, It is not good
that the man should be alone; I will
make him an help meet for him.*
GENESIS 2:18

This promise to one man, Adam, is also a promise to
people in general—that in marriage they will find a
helper that is right for them. But for everyone—even
those men and women who never marry—God will
provide a Helper in His Holy Spirit (John 15:26),
who gives Christians the power they need to live
well (Galatians 5:22–23).

DAY 2

And thou Bethlehem, in the land of Juda,
art not the least among the princes of Juda:
for out of thee shall come a Governor,
that shall rule my people Israel.
MATTHEW 2:6

The Jewish leaders, in answering King Herod's question, were quoting the prophet Micah, who predicted Jesus' birth—and birthplace—more than seven hundred years earlier. You can be sure that when God makes a promise, He'll keep it!

DAY 3

GENESIS 5–7; MATTHEW 3; PSALM 3

But thou, O Lord,
art a shield for me; my glory,
and the lifter up of mine head.
Psalm 3:3

Like a mother chicken, wrapping her wings around her little ones (Matthew 23:37), God protects and cares for His own. Though we still experience troubles in this world—accidents, illnesses, ultimately death—we know that God will never leave us on our own (Hebrews 13:5), and He is preparing an eternal home for us (John 14:2).

DAY 4

GENESIS 8–10; MATTHEW 4; PSALM 4

But [Jesus] answered and said,
It is written, Man shall not live by bread alone,
but by every word that proceedeth
out of the mouth of God.
MATTHEW 4:4

Want to find real life? It's in the living and powerful Word of God (Hebrews 4:12). You need bread to feed your body, but the Bible gives strength to your soul and spirit. You're now in the fourth day of a one-year "diet" of God's Word—stay with it! This is where you'll find the life worth living.

DAY 5

*Now the Lord had said unto Abram, Get thee
out of thy country, and from thy kindred, and from
thy father's house, unto a land that I will shew thee:
and I will make of thee a great nation, and I
will bless thee, and make thy name great;
and thou shalt be a blessing.*
Genesis 12:1–2

Over some four thousand years, God has proven that
His promises are good. God changed Abram's name,
which means "honored father," to *Abraham*—"father
of many"—and Abraham is the forefather of the
Jewish people. But he's also the father of those
who believe God by faith (Romans 4:16)—a great
heavenly nation from among all the people of earth!

DAY 6

But I say unto you, Love your enemies, bless them that curse you, do good to them that hate you, and pray for them which despitefully use you, and persecute you; that ye may be the children of your Father which is in heaven.
MATTHEW 5:44–45

If you want to be sure you're saved, Jesus gives a test in this verse: Are you praying for those people who treat you badly? If you are, Jesus says you're a son (or daughter) of the heavenly Father. It's not always easy, humanly speaking, but God has also promised that "my strength is made perfect in weakness" (2 Corinthians 12:9).

DAY 7

God judgeth the righteous.
PSALM 7:11

We live in an unfair world. The wealthy and powerful seem to work the system to their own ends, leaving the rest of us craving justice. But the psalm writer promises that God's judgments are right and sure. Since God knows everything (1 John 3:20), He can decide who's right, who's wrong, and what's best. Be faithful—and trust Him with the end result.

DAY 8

GENESIS 19–20; MATTHEW 6:19–34; PSALM 8

*But seek ye first the kingdom of God,
and his righteousness; and all these
things shall be added unto you.*
MATTHEW 6:33

Sometimes life seems incomplete unless we have something to worry about. What will happen if. . . ? What am I going to do about. . . ? How can I afford. . . ? In Matthew 6, Jesus offers a simple dose of reality: God feeds the birds and dresses the grass. Of course He's going to provide for His children. So don't worry—trust.

DAY 9

──── BIBLE READING: ────

GENESIS 21–23; MATTHEW 7:1–11; PSALM 9:1–8

*And the Lord visited Sarah as he had said,
and the Lord did unto Sarah as he had spoken.*
GENESIS 21:1

Crazy as it seemed, ninety-year-old Sarah was having a baby. Why? Because God had promised her husband, Abraham, that he would become the father of a great nation—and God always keeps His promises, even those that may seem impossible. Or, in God's own words, "Is any thing too hard for the Lord?" (Genesis 18:14).

DAY 10

Therefore whosoever heareth these sayings of mine, and doeth them, I will liken him unto a wise man, which built his house upon a rock.
MATTHEW 7:24

God doesn't want you to simply be a silent partner. To have a faith that's lasting, you can't just talk the talk. . .you've got to walk the talk. The apostle James puts it another way: "But be ye doers of the word, and not hearers only, deceiving your own selves" (James 1:22). God promises your faith will be stronger if you really live your life for Him.

DAY 11

— BIBLE READING: —

GENESIS 25–26; MATTHEW 8:1–17; PSALM 10:1–11

That it might be fulfilled which was spoken by Esaias the prophet, saying, Himself took our infirmities, and bare our sicknesses.
MATTHEW 8:17

Sickness, the death of a loved one, the loss of a job, marital problems. . . As Christians, we all struggle with faith in those trying times of our lives. It's not always easy to give up control to God. But He has promised to care for us—always. Remember that God will never forsake you (Hebrews 13:5), and hold fast to faith. If God says it, He'll do it!

DAY 12

GENESIS 27:1–28:9; MATTHEW 8:18–34; PSALM 10:12–18

*Thou hast seen it; for thou beholdest mischief
and spite, to requite it with thy hand:
the poor committeth himself unto thee;
thou art the helper of the fatherless.*
PSALM 10:14

As Creator, heavenly Father, Savior, and Lord, God is the most versatile character on the stage of life. When an important player in life—a mom, a dad, a mentor, a friend—is missing, God steps in and knows all the right lines and cues. The truth is, human relationships fail to meet expectations. A relationship with God will never fall short of the mark.

DAY 13

And, behold, the LORD stood above it, and said,
I am the LORD God of Abraham thy father,
and the God of Isaac: the land whereon thou liest,
to thee will I give it, and to thy seed.
GENESIS 28:13

Ever wonder why the tiny nation of Israel—about the size and population of Massachusetts—is such a focal point for world events? Today's verse helps to explain. God promised Jacob (later renamed "Israel") that his family would always have claim to land in the Middle East. Though for centuries many have fought these "chosen people" (Deuteronomy 10:15), Israel's presence proves God's faithfulness.

DAY 14

GENESIS 30:1–31:21; MATTHEW 10:1–15; PSALM 12

Thou shalt keep them, O LORD,
thou shalt preserve them from this
generation for ever.
PSALM 12:7

Our world is overflowing with temptations, which constantly try to lay claim to our hearts and minds. We can rejoice in knowing that our Lord and Savior has provided us with His protection and strength when our human desires threaten to take over, when our own strength just isn't enough. He is faithful (2 Thessalonians 3:3)!

DAY 15

—— BIBLE READING: ——

GENESIS 31:22–32:21; MATTHEW 10:16–36; PSALM 13

*Whosoever therefore shall confess me before
men, him will I confess also before my
Father which is in heaven.*
MATTHEW 10:32

It's a simple, give-and-take transaction. Tell others
about Jesus on earth and Jesus tells His Father in
heaven. Harvesting the fruit of sharing Christ with
others may seem like its own reward, but Jesus
offers more. Like a proud parent, He brags on His
followers for an everlasting reward.

DAY 16

──── BIBLE READING: ────

GENESIS 32:22–34:31; MATTHEW 10:37–11:6; PSALM 14

He that findeth his life shall lose it:
and he that loseth his life for
my sake shall find it.
MATTHEW 10:39

Here is a paradox—a seemingly contradictory statement. But Jesus wasn't just playing with words. He knew that real life—life in the Spirit on earth, life forever in heaven—comes only when people surrender everything to Him. "I am the way, the truth, and the life," Jesus said (John 14:6). His new life (1 Corinthians 15:22) is better than anything we could lose!

DAY 17

— BIBLE READING: —
GENESIS 35–36; MATTHEW 11:7–24; PSALM 15

Lord, who shall abide in thy tabernacle?
Who shall dwell in thy holy hill? He that
walketh uprightly, and worketh righteousness,
and speaketh the truth in his heart.
PSALM 15:1–2

Christlike. This word brings to mind the ultimate goal of the Christian life—to be more like Jesus every day. While we'll never be perfect because of our sinful human nature, we can strive for righteous living . . .taking a stand for what's good and acceptable in God's sight (Romans 12:2). Then we can enjoy an ever-growing, intimate relationship with Christ—for life!

DAY 18

*Come unto me, all ye that labour and are
heavy laden, and I will give you rest.*
MATTHEW 11:28

Life has a way of dragging down, tiring out, and frustrating even the most able-bodied people. Relationships, careers, responsibilities, burdens, and unexpected troubles weigh heavily on hearts and minds, often pulling committed believers away from building a relationship with Christ. But He knows we're busy, overworked, and tired. That's why He promises us rest—more satisfying than the best nap ever—if we simply go to Him.

DAY 19

Behold my servant, whom I have chosen;
my beloved, in whom my soul is well pleased:
I will put my spirit upon him, and he
shall shew judgment to the Gentiles.
MATTHEW 12:18

Good parents give their children boundaries—a clear understanding of what should and shouldn't be done. God did the same for everyone through Jesus. Today's verse, a quotation from the Old Testament's book of Isaiah (42:1), describes One who will help the world understand right and wrong. Many won't accept Jesus' teaching, but those of us who do can enjoy the protection of God's perfect boundaries.

DAY 20

——— BIBLE READING: ———

GENESIS 41; MATTHEW 12:30–50; PSALM 18:1–15

*For whosoever shall do the will of my Father
which is in heaven, the same is my
brother, and sister, and mother.*
MATTHEW 12:50

When we take time to walk in Jesus' steps, we can feel closer to Him than ever before. We don't have to earn a degree in theology or travel to a remote mission outpost to be part of Jesus' family. Such a small gesture as giving someone a drink of cold water (Matthew 10:42) is worthy of blessing. Jesus said, "Freely ye have received, freely give" (Matthew 10:8).

DAY 21

— BIBLE READING: —

GENESIS 42–43; MATTHEW 13:1–9; PSALM 18:16–29

For thou wilt light my candle:
the LORD my God will enlighten my darkness.
PSALM 18:28

Life often seems too hard, and maybe occasionally even downright hopeless. When your light seems to be growing dim in the shadows of sin and sorrow, look up. Our Lord is the only real source of joy and hope there is. Lean on Him; He will keep your light burning bright.

DAY 22

For whosoever hath, to him shall be given,
and he shall have more abundance:
but whosoever hath not, from him
shall be taken away even that he hath.
MATTHEW 13:12

The disciples once asked Jesus why He liked to speak in parables—picture-stories with hidden meanings. Jesus' answer was a promise of spiritual insight for anyone who truly knows Him. When we believe in Jesus, God gives us a supernatural ability to understand the Bible and apply it to our lives. And it's not just a *little* ability, it's more than enough for the job. That's always the way God gives—over and above.

DAY 23

GENESIS 46:1–47:26; MATTHEW 13:24–43; PSALM 19

*The law of the LORD is perfect, converting the
soul: the testimony of the LORD is sure,
making wise the simple.*
PSALM 19:7

This world can be a depressing place, with daily
reports of wars, disasters, and terrorism. Sometimes
it's just as bad on the personal level, as people struggle
with finances, disease, and relationships. But God
promises a safe haven, a place to find new strength for
the soul: His Word. The Bible is "quick, and powerful"
(Hebrews 4:12). Take advantage of its benefits today!

DAY 24

—— BIBLE READING: ——

GENESIS 47:27–49:28; MATTHEW 13:44–58; PSALM 20

*Now know I that the LORD saveth his anointed;
he will hear him from his holy heaven with
the saving strength of his right hand.*
PSALM 20:6

We trust our friends. We trust our spouses. We trust our coworkers. We trust people who will inevitably let us down from time to time. Imagine how much more we can lean on our Savior, who keeps every one of His promises to us! Start today and put your trust in the only One who guarantees He'll never disappoint you—that's a promise!

DAY 25

And Joseph said unto his brethren, I die:
and God will surely visit you, and bring you
out of this land unto the land which he sware
to Abraham, to Isaac, and to Jacob.
GENESIS 50:24

The sons of Jacob didn't deserve the kind treatment their brother Joseph extended to them. After selling Joseph into Egyptian slavery and telling Jacob his beloved son was dead, Joseph's brothers folded their arms in smug pride of getting rid of the favored child. But later, after Joseph saved the entire family from famine and certain death, Joseph even went as far as to assure his family that God would indeed take care of them—the same way He takes care of His children today.

DAY 26

*And God heard their groaning, and God
remembered his covenant with Abraham,
with Isaac, and with Jacob.*
EXODUS 2:24

Under Joseph, the Jewish slave boy turned ruler, Egypt welcomed the people of Israel. But when a new king made life hard for the Jews, they cried to God—and He remembered His agreement with Abraham, Isaac, and Jacob. In time, God would lead the people back to their own land, just as He'd promised. Today, be sure that He'll also remember the promises He's made to *you*.

DAY 27

BIBLE READING:

EXODUS 4:1–5:21; MATTHEW 15:29–16:12; PSALM 22:22–31

For he hath not despised nor abhorred the affliction of the afflicted; neither hath he hid his face from him; but when he cried unto him, he heard.
PSALM 22:24

Have you ever turned your eyes and heart away from someone in need? Have you ever ignored a plea for help? Follow Jesus' example from today's scripture, and listen to the cries of those who are hurting. Whether you are able to give financial or emotional support, or even just a few hours of your time, you're promised to be blessed for your efforts.

DAY 28

EXODUS 5:22–7:24; MATTHEW 16:13–28; PSALM 23

*And I say also unto thee, That thou art Peter,
and upon this rock I will build my church;
and the gates of hell shall not prevail against it.*
MATTHEW 16:18

During His ministry, Jesus Christ laid the groundwork for the kingdom of God on earth—the Church. His disciples, although devoted to their leader, must have looked at one another with skepticism that such an institution could be built on their shoulders. But Jesus promises more than an organization of believers. Someday, when all other earthly institutions fail, Christ's Church will live on.

DAY 29

And Pharaoh said, I will let you go, that ye may sacrifice to the LORD your God in the wilderness.
EXODUS 8:28

Here's an example of a human promise—the kind you *can't* count on. The king of Egypt said he would let Moses and the people of Israel leave their slavery, but then he changed his mind. Isn't it nice to know that God never goes back on a promise? "God is not a man, that he should lie; neither the son of man, that he should repent: hath he said, and shall he not do it? or hath he spoken, and shall he not make it good?" (Numbers 23:19).

DAY 30

*Mine eyes are ever toward the L*ORD*;*
for he shall pluck my feet out of the net.
PSALM 25:15

Today, while we don't think of our feet being tangled in a net, we *can* imagine being stuck in a rut, going nowhere fast, or getting caught up in the rat race. Whatever the euphemism, our lives are truly hopeless without the knowledge of Jesus' saving grace and the hope of eternal life. Keep your eyes on Jesus, knowing He has a plan for you (Hebrews 12:1–2).

DAY 31

BIBLE READING:
EXODUS 12; MATTHEW 18:1-20; PSALM 26

For the Son of man is come to
save that which was lost.
MATTHEW 18:11

Never has a greater gift been given, the gift of God's Son. . .who was sent to save us from sin and to offer eternal life (John 3:16). He was sent to save the "lost." We don't have to be perfect and sin-free. We can't purchase eternal life, because it's a gift freely given. All we need to do is believe God's promise and accept this gift. It doesn't get any easier than that!

DAY 32

BIBLE READING:

EXODUS 13–14; MATTHEW 18:21–35; PSALM 27

*When my father and my mother forsake me,
then the Lord will take me up.*
PSALM 27:10

Earthly relationships often fall apart. Families separate. Parents abandon their children. Friends come and go. But we need not ever feel lost and forgotten. We have the Lord, who will always be close to our hearts. A Father who will always listen, always support, always care. Lean on Him, and you'll never be lonely. That's a promise!

DAY 33

BIBLE READING:
EXODUS 15–16; MATTHEW 19:1–15; PSALM 28

*For this cause shall a man leave father
and mother, and shall cleave to his wife:
and they twain shall be one flesh.*
MATTHEW 19:5

God's promise for marriage is that it will be unlike any other relationship between two people. The Bible describes friendship or brotherhood as being *near* one another (Proverbs 18:24). But in a marriage, husband and wife are not just joined, they experience a oneness in Christ. Think of it as preparation for perfect harmony with God that's only attainable in eternity.

DAY 34

— BIBLE READING: —

EXODUS 17–19; MATTHEW 19:16–30; PSALM 29

*But Jesus beheld them, and said unto them,
With men this is impossible; but with
God all things are possible.*
MATTHEW 19:26

Forget silly questions like, "Can God create a rock so big that He can't lift it?" God won't ever do anything that goes against His nature—but He can do anything that benefits you as His child. "If ye then, being evil, know how to give good gifts unto your children," Jesus once said, "how much more shall your heavenly Father give the Holy Spirit to them that ask him?" (Luke 11:13).

DAY 35

And shewing mercy unto thousands of them that love me, and keep my commandments.
EXODUS 20:6

Ever been asked what makes you seem so different? Why you're able to get through tough times without breaking? Share the good news that Christ has blessed you and that He makes it possible to have joy in *all* stages of life—even the not-so-good times. When you serve the Lord, your light will shine (Matthew 5:16), and His delight will bring abundant blessings to you. So much that others will take notice.

DAY 36

—— BIBLE READING: ——
EXODUS 22–23; MATTHEW 20:20–34; PSALM 31:1–8

And whosoever will be chief among you,
let him be your servant.
MATTHEW 20:27

Jesus leads the campaign for upside-down, topsy-turvy, counterintuitive rules for His kingdom. Instead of the best getting first dibs, it's the lowliest among His followers—those willing to serve others the same way Christ served—that will one day earn a place of honor in eternity.

DAY 37

EXODUS 24–25; MATTHEW 21:1-27; PSALM 31:9-18

*And all things, whatsoever ye shall
ask in prayer, believing, ye shall receive.*
MATTHEW 21:22

Faith connects us to God. When we really believe
in who He is and what He's promised, He responds
with all the power in the universe—because
that's exactly what God is. When our faith-filled
prayers align with His desires, look out. Amazing
things are about to happen!

DAY 38

O love the Lord, all ye his saints:
for the Lord preserveth the faithful.
PSALM 31:23

Walk beside the Lord, and you'll reap the benefits of serving Him. He'll reward you if you earnestly seek Him (Hebrews 11:6). He'll give you what you ask for in prayer (Matthew 21:22). He'll bless your life (John 20:29). Be faithful, and you're sure to experience an amazing life—guaranteed.

DAY 39

I acknowledge my sin unto thee,
and mine iniquity have I not hid. I said,
I will confess my transgressions unto the LORD;
and thou forgavest the iniquity of my sin.
PSALM 32:5

God's forgiveness offers much more than removal of sin. In addition to wiping clean a repenting sinner's slate, He removes the guilt of the offense. Just think— it isn't necessary to dwell on, regret, or stew about forgiven sin. It's God's guarantee—designed to calm His children's spirits and to bless their lives.

DAY 40

The counsel of the LORD standeth for ever,
the thoughts of his heart to all generations.
PSALM 33:11

"I've had a change of plans." Is there anyone who has *never* spoken those words or had them spoken to them? Human life is all about change—but God offers beautiful security in His never-changing plans. Like what? How about Jesus' plans on heaven: "And if I go and prepare a place for you, I will come again, and receive you unto myself; that where I am, there ye may be also" (John 14:3).

DAY 41

Six days may work be done; but in the seventh is the sabbath of rest, holy to the LORD. . .for in six days the LORD made heaven and earth, and on the seventh day he rested, and was refreshed.
EXODUS 31:15, 17

Rest is an important concept in the Bible. Besides God's example after Creation, we read about the land needing a rest from constant planting (Leviticus 25:5) and Jesus needing to rest after dealing with throngs of people (Mark 6:31). God knows that when we rest, when we are still, we are most able to sense His presence in our lives. Spend some time resting in God's promise today.

DAY 42

BIBLE READING:

EXODUS 32–33; MATTHEW 24:29–51; PSALM 34:1–7

I sought the LORD, and he heard me,
and delivered me from all my fears.
PSALM 34:4

Give honor and glory to God by placing your worries at His feet. He alone offers all the comfort and assurance we need for whatever we're facing in our lives. Without Him, we'd be anxious, we'd be afraid, we'd be hopeless. . .but with Him, we can be at peace, knowing He is all we'll ever need. He will give us rest from the burdens of life (Matthew 11:28).

DAY 43

BIBLE READING:

EXODUS 34:1–35:29; MATTHEW 25:1–13; PSALM 34:8–22

Watch therefore, for ye know neither the day nor the hour wherein the Son of man cometh.
MATTHEW 25:13

Humans thrive on being in control. Schedules, agendas, and calendars can spell out every minute of every day. But Jesus Christ left the date and time of His return a mystery. The Son Himself doesn't even know when He'll make His next earthly appearance (Matthew 24:36). Christians shouldn't take this uncertainty and push the panic button. Instead, consider waiting in expectant anticipation, preparing each day as though Jesus will return.

DAY 44

── BIBLE READING: ──
EXODUS 35:30–37:29; MATTHEW 25:14–30;
PSALM 35:1–8

*Draw out also the spear, and stop the
way against them that persecute me:
say unto my soul, I am thy salvation.*
PSALM 35:3

The psalm writer was upset. Enemies were pursuing him with murder on their minds. But the ancient poet knew just where to find deliverance: from the one true God, the only One able to save. Times and circumstances have changed since this psalm was written, but God is still in the saving business. "As ye have therefore received Christ Jesus the Lord, so walk ye in him" (Colossians 2:6).

DAY 45

— BIBLE READING: —

EXODUS 38–39; MATTHEW 25:31–46; PSALM 35:9–17

And the King shall answer and say unto them,
Verily I say unto you, Inasmuch as ye have done
it unto one of the least of these my brethren,
ye have done it unto me.
MATTHEW 25:40

God calls on us to love one another—just as He loves us (John 13:34). Today's scripture tells us more about loving those who may not be living up to our standards in the world. For every deed of kindness, every hand reached out in love, comes the reminder that we are reflecting these actions onto Christ. Loving others—even those who are unlovable to the rest of the world—delights our heavenly Father. Let your light shine!

DAY 46

BIBLE READING:

EXODUS 40; MATTHEW 26:1-35; PSALM 35:18-28

For this is my blood of the new testament,
which is shed for many for the remission of sins.
MATTHEW 26:28

Countless songs and poems have been written about the blood of Jesus. The beauty of forgiveness through Christ's blood is undeniable—yet the pain, suffering, and sacrifice He experienced shouldn't be overlooked. Jesus of Nazareth was a man of flesh and bones just like us. His painful death would have been worth it to Him, even if only one person ever accepted the gift.

DAY 47

*Jesus saith unto him, Thou hast said: nevertheless
I say unto you, Hereafter shall ye see the Son
of man sitting on the right hand of power,
and coming in the clouds of heaven.*
MATTHEW 26:64

Here is one of the most exciting promises in all of
God's Word: Jesus is coming again! Once He came
to earth quietly, as a helpless baby in a small-town
stable. But the day is coming when He'll reappear as
a powerful King. When will that be? It's a surprise,
according to Jesus Himself: "Watch therefore: for
ye know not what hour your Lord doth come"
(Matthew 24:42).

DAY 48

LEVITICUS 4:1–5:13; MATTHEW 26:69–27:26; PSALM 36:7–12

They shall be abundantly satisfied with the fatness of thy house; and thou shalt make them drink of the river of thy pleasures.
PSALM 36:8

If your heart's lacking joy today, drink deep from God's promise. Just knowing that He holds our lives in the palm of His hand is reason enough to rejoice— no matter what the day might bring. Thank Him for His mercy and His everlasting goodness. Nothing else in the world can bring joy into our lives like He can.

DAY 49

BIBLE READING:

LEVITICUS 5:14–7:21; MATTHEW 27:27–50; PSALM 37:1–6

Delight thyself also in the LORD: and he shall give thee the desires of thine heart.
PSALM 37:4

Ask a child to make a Christmas list and he won't struggle to come up with a lengthy collection of wants. Adults also have a hard time distinguishing between needs and wants. It's easy to read Psalm 37:4 to mean Christians get whatever they want—making God little more than a glorified Santa Claus. But it's much more than that. "Delighting in the Lord" means allowing His perfect wisdom to transform a heart desire to what ultimately brings His kingdom to earth.

DAY 50

BIBLE READING:
LEVITICUS 7:22–8:36; MATTHEW 27:51–66; PSALM 37:7–26

For yet a little while, and the wicked shall not be:
yea, thou shalt diligently consider his
place, and it shall not be.
Psalm 37:10

"The sinful man" has caused plenty of trouble in our world—terrorism, child abuse, murder, even the business scandals that wipe out jobs and retirement funds. But the psalm writer knew a day was coming when God would take every evil influence out of the picture. In "a little while," from God's eternal viewpoint, sin will be gone—replaced by the perfection of heaven (Revelation 21:4).

DAY 51

—— BIBLE READING: ——
LEVITICUS 9–10; MATTHEW 28; PSALM 37:27–40

*And the angel answered and said unto the women,
Fear not ye: for I know that ye seek Jesus, which
was crucified. He is not here: for he is risen, as he
said. Come, see the place where the Lord lay.*
MATTHEW 28:5–6

Of all the promises in the Bible, surely none is more
treasured than Jesus' assurance that He would rise
from the dead. Because Jesus conquered death,
we too will live forever with Him—if only we believe
that He is God's Son. Want to dispel those winter
blues? Start your day by praising God for His most
wonderful Son. . .and know that one day you'll
meet Him face-to-face.

DAY 52

For in thee, O Lord, do I hope:
thou wilt hear, O Lord my God.
PSALM 38:15

Waiting. . . It's not easy to wait for an answer to prayer. Sometimes we feel like we've been placed on hold—or maybe God has even forgotten our request. We can rest assured that He *will* answer our prayer—God's Word says we just need to be patient (Psalm 37:7). He knows what's best for us. His timing—even though it may not be what we had in mind—is always perfect.

DAY 53

And now, Lord, what wait I for? my hope is in thee.
Psalm 39:7

Nothing on earth is certain. Plans can be made, provisions supplied, money saved, and schedules penned, but none of these is guaranteed. The healthiest relationship can fail, and leaders fall from grace. When everything seems to crumble, count on hope in God—the Author, Savior, and Friend above all. His plan for eternity is a guarantee for Christians.

DAY 54

*When Jesus saw their faith, he said unto the sick
of the palsy, Son, thy sins be forgiven thee.*
MARK 2:5

Two thousand years ago, Jesus made this life-changing promise to a man with a great need. He's still speaking those words. "If we confess our sins, he is faithful and just to forgive us our sins, and to cleanse us from all unrighteousness," the apostle John wrote (1 John 1:9). With our sins forgiven, we are truly God's sons and daughters, enjoying all the benefits of that wonderful relationship.

DAY 55

*For whosoever shall do the will of God,
the same is my brother, and my sister, and mother.*
MARK 3:35

A member of Jesus' family. That's what He calls you if you are a follower of God. You belong to a much larger family than that of your father, mother, sisters, and brothers. You are a part of a body (a *family*) of believers (Romans 12:5)—your "brothers" and "sisters" in Christ. Today, celebrate and thank the Lord for this extended family.

DAY 56

Blessed is he that considereth the poor:
the Lord will deliver him in time of trouble.
PSALM 41:1

Jesus had a special place in His heart for the earth's poor. Throughout His earthly ministry He urged His followers to take care of the less fortunate, clothe the bare, and feed the hungry. Here the psalm writer says that caring for the poor not only brings happiness, but that the Lord promises the giver a safety net during the rough patches of life.

DAY 57

Ye shall therefore keep my statutes,
and my judgments: which if a man do,
he shall live in them: I am the LORD.
LEVITICUS 18:5

Why, some people ask, does God have so many rules? Is He trying to take away all our fun? Hardly. God's laws are designed both to honor Him and to protect us. Compare today's Old Testament passage with the realities of the modern world—pornography, AIDS, sexual abuse, broken families. Can anyone honestly argue that God's ways are too restrictive?

DAY 58

Yet the LORD will command his lovingkindness in the day time, and in the night his song shall be with me, and my prayer unto the God of my life.
PSALM 42:8

A friend, a faithful companion, a loving Father—24-7. He's by your side, offering you His comfort, His kindness, His mercy. . . . There isn't a moment, day or night, that He'll leave you on your own. No matter what time of day, you can go to Him in prayer and He'll be ready to listen, wrapping His loving arms around you.

DAY 59

Through thee will we push down our enemies:
through thy name will we tread them
under that rise up against us.
PSALM 44:5

God doesn't promise a life free of enemies. Jesus tells His followers in Matthew 5:44 to "Love your enemies, bless them that curse you, do good to them that hate you, and pray for them which despitefully use you, and persecute you." He even guarantees persecution to Christians (Matthew 24:9). But these promises aren't all doom and gloom. The heavenly Father says His followers will be able to overcome their enemies in ultimate victory—victory that was sealed when Jesus gave His life on the cross.

DAY 60

*And [Herod] sware unto her, Whatsoever thou
shalt ask of me, I will give it thee,
unto the half of my kingdom.*
MARK 6:23

Here's a foolish promise—one that cost a king his honor and a prophet his life. The king, Herod Antipas, made this offer to his stepdaughter, who had performed a pleasing dance. The girl asked her mother, Herodias, what to request—and the queen, angry at John the Baptist's criticism of her marriage to Herod, demanded the prophet's head. Though few of us have power like Herod, we still need to be careful what we promise. Careless words can create much pain.

DAY 61

Thy throne, O God, is for ever and ever:
the sceptre of thy kingdom is a right sceptre.
PSALM 45:6

Disposable products have simplified the lives of millions of people. From razors to forks and diapers to pens, when an object has run its course or usefulness, it's simply discarded and never thought of again. God's rule in the universe is the exact opposite. His throne is forever. It existed before the world came into being and will remain into eternity. Take it as a comfort and a mind boggler, all wrapped in one.

DAY 62

─ BIBLE READING: ─

LEVITICUS 26; MARK 7; PSALM 45:13-17

And [Jesus] said unto her, For this saying go thy
way; the devil is gone out of thy daughter.
MARK 7:29

Jesus' promise to a desperate mother was fulfilled
instantly—and gives us a glimpse into God's heart
for needy people. This non-Jewish woman knew
Jesus could help her demon-possessed daughter,
but Jesus basically said His ministry was only for
the Jews. When the woman responded in humility,
rather than anger, Jesus' heart was moved—and He
gave her exactly what she asked for.

DAY 63

For whosoever will save his life shall lose it;
but whosoever shall lose his life for my sake and
the gospel's, the same shall save it. For what
shall it profit a man, if he shall gain the
whole world, and lose his own soul?
MARK 8:35–36

You can have everything in this world—wealth, fame, power—and have nothing. You can have nothing in this world—no wealth, no fame, no power—and have everything (Matthew 6:19–21). God tells us we are not to love the world or anything of the world (1 John 2:15). We are, instead, to rid ourselves of worldly things and focus on Christ and the Good News, the only things that matter now. . .and for eternity.

DAY 64

For the LORD most high is terrible; he is a great King over all the earth. . . . For the shields of the earth belong unto God: he is greatly exalted.
PSALM 47:2, 9

It's sometimes hard to think of the whole earth as being a single entity. With wars, feuding factions, and different ideologies, it often seems as though disunity rules the world. But the truth is, there is One who rules over all, whether we all acknowledge His kingship or not. Everything and everyone—from the greatest natural disaster and the most powerful world leader to the smallest grain of sand and lowliest servant—belongs to God.

DAY 65

───── BIBLE READING: ─────

NUMBERS 3; MARK 9:14–50; PSALM 48:1–8

*For [Jesus] taught his disciples, and said unto them,
The Son of man is delivered into the hands of
men, and they shall kill him; and after that
he is killed, he shall rise the third day.*
MARK 9:31

Amazing is a good word to describe this promise.
Jesus said He would die and then come back to
life. . .and He did! Many people saw that promise
fulfilled, according to the apostle Paul: Peter, the
twelve disciples, more than five hundred believers
at one time (1 Corinthians 15:5–6). Though we
as Christians can't see Jesus today, we too know He's
alive—by the work He does in our hearts.

DAY 66

——— BIBLE READING: ———
NUMBERS 4; MARK 10:1-34; PSALM 48:9-14

And Jesus looking upon them saith,
With men it is impossible, but not with
God: for with God all things are possible.
MARK 10:27

Throughout our lifetimes, we may be plagued by many troubles. Sickness. Sin. Unemployment. Divorce. Childlessness. The list goes on and on. While we can't rely on people to fix our problems, there is One we can depend on to help get us through when life seems hopeless. God is still in the miracle-working business. Call out to Him today.

DAY 67

*For even the Son of man came not to be
ministered unto, but to minister; and to
give his life a ransom for many.*
MARK 10:45

Many dignitaries and celebrities are used to being cared for. From an army of servants to outrageous demands at personal appearances, it seems the more money and notoriety a person possesses, the more he or she is pampered. Jesus didn't hold that same notion of entitlement. Not only did He shy away from celebrity, His demonstrated purpose was one of servanthood and care for others.

DAY 68

The LORD lift up his countenance
upon thee, and give thee peace.
NUMBERS 6:26

Here is God's own blessing for His own people—
the ancient Israelites. Aaron the priest was to say
these words over the people, calling down God's
goodness on them. Today, with Jesus as our High
Priest (Hebrews 4:14), we too enjoy all the goodness
of God. "To the praise of the glory of his grace," Paul
wrote in Ephesians 1:6, "wherein he hath made us
accepted in the beloved."

DAY 69

BIBLE READING:

NUMBERS 7:48–8:4; MARK 12:1–27; PSALM 50:1–15

I know all the fowls of the mountains:
and the wild beasts of the field are mine.
PSALM 50:11

Our God is an all-knowing, all-seeing Creator. Everything in the world was created by Him and is precious to Him. Do you know that He even knows how many hairs you have on your head (Matthew 10:30)? Serving a sovereign Lord should give us confidence to share our faith with others and say with the writer of Hebrews, "I will not fear what man shall do unto me" (Hebrews 13:6).

DAY 70

Whoso offereth praise glorifieth me: and to him that ordereth his conversation aright will I shew the salvation of God.
PSALM 50:23

Have you said a prayer of thanks lately? It's easy to get into the rut of "I need. . . ," "I want. . ." prayers. But what about those things God has blessed you with in life? Your family, your friends, your job, your home. . .God has given you all these things and more. Be sure to thank Him. He'll be delighted to hear from you.

DAY 71

Against thee, thee only, have I sinned, and done this evil in thy sight: that thou mightest be justified when thou speakest, and be clear when thou judgest.
PSALM 51:4

It's sometimes difficult for children to accept the direction of a parent—God's children are no exception—but the heavenly Father has parenting figured out. He's always right and always fair. Although His followers may not always understand God's answers or decisions, that doesn't change the fact that He was right yesterday, is right today, and will be right tomorrow.

DAY 72

——— BIBLE READING: ———
NUMBERS 12–13; MARK 13:9–37; PSALM 51:10–19

And ye shall be hated of all men for my name's sake.
MARK 13:13

Hold on, now. . .that's not a *nice* promise. Is Jesus really saying that following Him will make people hate us? Well, yes. You don't have to look far to find people who criticize, mock, and slander our Christian faith. But Jesus (a) gave us fair warning, and (b) promises great reward for staying true to Him (Matthew 5:11–12).

DAY 73

——— BIBLE READING: ———
NUMBERS 14; MARK 14:1-31; PSALM 52

The LORD is longsuffering, and of great mercy,
forgiving iniquity and transgression.
NUMBERS 14:18

Ever do something you shouldn't and as a result feel as though you aren't worthy of God's love and mercy? God's love for us never wavers—not even when we're at our worst. What a blessing to know that when we mess up, God will forgive us in an instant. All we need to do is ask (1 John 1:9).

DAY 74

— BIBLE READING: —

NUMBERS 15; MARK 14:32–72; PSALM 53

*But he held his peace, and answered nothing.
Again the high priest asked him, and said unto
him, Art thou the Christ, the Son of the Blessed?
And Jesus said, I am: and ye shall see the Son
of man sitting on the right hand of power,
and coming in the clouds of heaven.*
MARK 14:61–62

Jesus never denied that He is the Messiah. He even
spent much of His ministry telling and retelling His
followers that He is the Savior of mankind. Although
the statement was powerful during His ministry,
none packed more punch than standing in front of
the high priest and announcing Himself as the Son
of God who will someday come again.

DAY 75

Behold, God is mine helper: the Lord is with them that uphold my soul.
PSALM 54:4

Even the richest, strongest, and most intelligent people sometimes need help. The more average among us probably need even more. What better helper than God Himself? The One who created the universe and keeps it running (Colossians 1:16–17), the One who knows everything (Psalm 147:5), the One who loved you enough to send His Son to die on the cross (John 3:16)—He's more than enough for any problem you face!

DAY 76

BIBLE READING:
NUMBERS 17–18; MARK 15:33–47; PSALM 55

Cast thy burden upon the L ORD,
and he shall sustain thee: he shall never
suffer the righteous to be moved.
PSALM 55:22

Life is hard. We come face-to-face with some pretty tough stuff as we journey through the years—difficult relationships, sickness, stress, the death of a loved one—things that leave us feeling weak and hopeless. We don't need to bear these burdens alone. God wants us to give our worries and cares to Him (Matthew 11:28). He'll offer up just the strength we need to make it through.

DAY 77

And [the angel] saith unto them, Be not affrighted:
Ye seek Jesus of Nazareth, which was crucified:
he is risen; he is not here: behold the
place where they laid him.
Mark 16:6

Some of Jesus Christ's promises are yet to be fulfilled: His second coming, the completion of heaven. His resurrection, in comparison to some of His other promises, was an instant-gratification kind of promise. Christ's rising from the dead shook His believers and the rest of the world to the core. How much more amazing will His return be?

DAY 78

And the Lord said unto Moses, Make thee a fiery serpent, and set it upon a pole: and it shall come to pass, that every one that is bitten, when he looketh upon it, shall live.
NUMBERS 21:8

The ancient Israelites were in trouble—their complaining had caused God to punish them with poisonous snakes. But when they admitted their sin, God promised a way of escape—and gave a hint of Jesus' perfect sacrifice to come. Like the brass snake, Jesus would be lifted up on a long piece of wood. And by looking to Jesus, we too can live.

DAY 79

*And [Balaam] took up his parable, and said,
Rise up, Balak, and hear; hearken unto me,
thou son of Zippor: God is not a man, that he
should lie; neither the son of man, that he should
repent: hath he said, and shall he not do it? or
hath he spoken, and shall he not make it good?*
NUMBERS 23:18–19

Often our prayer time can seem so casual that we
imagine God more like a best friend than the Author
of our salvation (Hebrews 12:2). Yet by His Word
the world was made (2 Peter 3:5), and by His Word
we have eternal life (John 6:68). How comforting
to know He has promised that His Word will never
pass away (Matthew 24:35)!

DAY 80

*For unto you is born this day in the city of David
a Saviour, which is Christ the Lord.*
LUKE 2:11

No other gift ever given could rival the gift God sent on that Christmas night so long ago. What excitement the shepherds must have felt at hearing the news of Christ's birth from the angels! Because God sent His Son to save us, we are freed from the punishment of sin and death and can have eternal life (John 3:16; 1 John 4:9)—no strings attached. All we need to do is believe and accept this amazing gift.

DAY 81

For mine eyes have seen thy salvation,
which thou hast prepared before the face
of all people; a light to lighten the Gentiles,
and the glory of thy people Israel.
LUKE 2:30–32

An inexpensive night-light may save a stubbed toe or a banged elbow in the darkness. Such a small and seemingly insignificant source of illumination means the difference between groggily stumbling through the unknown and being able to see the surroundings and maneuver through life. Jesus was sent to shine on every man, woman, and child who, otherwise, would flounder in the dark.

DAY 82

BIBLE READING:

NUMBERS 27:12–29:11; LUKE 2:39–52; PSALM 59:9–17

The God of my mercy shall prevent me: God shall let me see my desire upon mine enemies.
PSALM 59:10

From the giant Goliath, to the paranoid King Saul, to his own ambitious son Absalom, David the psalm writer had plenty of enemies. But David also knew he would win in the end. We can claim that promise too. Our enemies will either pay for their sins at the final judgment, or (preferably) they'll join us in the Christian faith. In the meantime, our job is to love them (Luke 6:27).

DAY 83

*John answered, saying unto them all, I indeed
baptize you with water; but one mightier than
I cometh, the latchet of whose shoes I am
not worthy to unloose: he shall baptize
you with the Holy Ghost and with fire.*
LUKE 3:16

These words, spoken by John the Baptist, prepared
the way for Jesus, as some of the people were
questioning and wondering whether John was the
promised Savior. Jesus came to earth—fully God
and fully man—to teach His followers the way to
salvation. Say a prayer of thanks to God today for
sending His Son.

DAY 84

*Through God we shall do valiantly: for he
it is that shall tread down our enemies.*
PSALM 60:12

Without God's help, humans accomplish nothing.
Without God's help, nothing makes sense, and
humans have no control over the way the chips
fall. With God's help, humans can find meaning,
knowing God's in control. Life can be frustrating,
confusing, and sometimes scary, but everything is in
His hands. Only with God's help can humans make
it through life, doing well.

DAY 85

And Jesus said unto Simon, Fear not;
from henceforth thou shalt catch men.
LUKE 5:10

For Peter, James, and John, fishing provided a living
. . .but Jesus provided a purpose. By changing
their job description to "fishers of men," Jesus gave
His disciples a task with eternal consequences. As
Christians today, we have the same job description.
Whether we're nurses or factory workers, salespeople
or police officers, president of the United States or a
stay-at-home mom, ultimately, we should be "fishers
of men."

DAY 86

My soul, wait thou only upon God;
for my expectation is from him.
PSALM 62:5

God is waiting for you to spend some quiet time with Him. Share what's on your heart—your needs, your hardships, your goals—and wait for Him to respond. Quiet your heart and your mind as you connect with Him. Wait patiently for Him (Psalm 37:7). He is always there to listen and to comfort you—He's the best Friend you could have.

DAY 87

——— BIBLE READING: ———
DEUTERONOMY 1:1–2:25; LUKE 5:33–6:11; PSALM 62:7–12

Trust in him at all times; ye people, pour out your heart before him: God is a refuge for us. Selah.
PSALM 62:8

As they grow, children find those safety nets—a blanket, a stuffed toy, a thumb to suck—that they need to help during the scary parts of life. Similarly, adults trying to cope with the things *they* dread may find themselves in a diversion addiction—movies, food, TV, music; or worse, gambling, drugs, affairs, pornography. God doesn't want His children to rely on such things to soothe the soul. Instead, He offers His arms as a safe haven from the trials of life.

DAY 88

*Ye shall not fear them: for the L*ORD
your God he shall fight for you.
DEUTERONOMY 3:22

To the ancient Israelites, God was a warrior, fighting for them as they entered the Promised Land. Though 1 John 4:8 tells us "God is love," He still has plenty of fight in Him. God is now directing an invisible war against evil powers, a universal battle that will end when Jesus, the King of kings and Lord of lords, crushes Satan and his followers as described in Revelation 19–20.

DAY 89

BIBLE READING:

DEUTERONOMY 4:15–5:22; LUKE 6:36–49; PSALM 63:6–11

Give, and it shall be given unto you; good measure, pressed down, and shaken together, and running over, shall men give into your bosom. For with the same measure that ye mete withal it shall be measured to you again.
LUKE 6:38

To all those who have given gifts with the idea of getting something in return: read Luke 14:12–14. Jesus said we should invite the least prosperous, the disabled, and the downtrodden to dinner, knowing that we'll be rewarded in heaven. God loves a cheerful giver, and He promises to bless us when we give to Him (Malachi 3:10).

DAY 90

BIBLE READING:

DEUTERONOMY 5:23–7:26; LUKE 7:1–17; PSALM 64:1–5

*Know therefore that the LORD thy God, he is God,
the faithful God, which keepeth covenant and
mercy with them that love him and keep his
commandments to a thousand generations.*
DEUTERONOMY 7:9

Promises are made. Promises are broken. We've all experienced the letdown of a broken promise. It hurts when you have an expectation, and a friend, a family member, or a coworker fails to follow through. What a comfort to know that we have a Father who keeps *all* His promises, a Friend who will never let you down—guaranteed.

DAY 91

— BIBLE READING: —
DEUTERONOMY 8-9; LUKE 7:18-35; PSALM 64:6-10

*And blessed is he, whosoever shall
not be offended in me.*
LUKE 7:23

Here's the recipe for a happy life: walk closely with
God and be confident in your relationship with Him.
Don't worry about the opinions of others who may
criticize your Christianity. They'll only steal your joy.
Instead, share God's promise of a joyful spirit with
others who want to know what's different about
your life. They'll be glad you did.

DAY 92

And [Jesus] said to the woman,
Thy faith hath saved thee; go in peace.
LUKE 7:50

Faith is one of those intangible "Christianese" words many believers struggle to wrap their arms around. It's easy to claim faith in an object, idea, or even God, but in Luke 7, it's not the woman's profession of faith that shows her commitment to Christ. In this setting it's her physical acts of humility—washing and drying and putting perfume on Jesus' feet—that are her outward show of faith.

DAY 93

—— BIBLE READING: ——
DEUTERONOMY 12-13; LUKE 8:4-21; PSALM 65:9-13

*But that on the good ground are they, which in an
honest and good heart, having heard the word,
keep it, and bring forth fruit with patience.*
LUKE 8:15

Jesus' story of seeds and soils describes the different
reactions of people who hear God's Word. Some
don't respond at all; others show interest but soon
fall away. But for those whose hearts are "good
ground," there's a wonderful promise: the Word in
their lives will bear "fruit," the spiritual fruit that
makes our lives full.

DAY 94

He ruleth by his power for ever;
his eyes behold the nations: let not the
rebellious exalt themselves. Selah.
PSALM 66:7

Watch the evening news or read the headlines of the paper, and you're sure to be depressed about the state of the world. War. Unrest. Terrorism. Suffering. Disease. Poverty. We can't possibly change the entire world through our own actions, but we can pray for the world. . .and God will hear us. He alone watches over *all* nations. We can place the problems of the world in His hands and know He holds complete control—today and in the days yet to come.

DAY 95

--- BIBLE READING: ---
DEUTERONOMY 16:9-18:22; LUKE 8:40-56; PSALM 66:8-15

*That which is altogether just shalt thou follow,
that thou mayest live, and inherit the land
which the LORD thy God giveth thee.*
DEUTERONOMY 16:20

Just as earthly parents have expectations of their children, so too does God expect certain things from His children. At the top of that list is a simple idea: do what is right. But God doesn't ask His followers to do right for right's sake. His request is to follow what is right, and only what is right—and this will result in an eternal reward.

DAY 96

When thou goest out to battle against thine enemies, and seest horses, and chariots, and a people more than thou, be not afraid of them: for the LORD thy God is with thee, which brought thee up out of the land of Egypt.

DEUTERONOMY 20:1

Here's another promise to ancient Jews that mirrors God's dealings with Christians today. "I am with you always," Jesus promised His followers, "even unto the end of the world" (Matthew 28:20). If you ever struggle with fear or loneliness, put bookmarks in your Bible at these two verses!

DAY 97

O let the nations be glad and sing for joy:
for thou shalt judge the people righteously,
and govern the nations upon earth. Selah.
PSALM 67:4

We live in an unfair world. Evil sometimes appears to triumph over good, and we're left feeling shortchanged. We can be thankful though that the final Judge over all is our merciful Lord—a fair Judge indeed. Praise the Lord for His mercy and truth, which we can always count on in our ever-changing world.

DAY 98

God setteth the solitary in families.
PSALM 68:6

Although God created humans to have fellowship with one another (Genesis 2:18), the fact remains that loneliness is real in a world with a population of more than seven billion people. God knew this would happen. His love offers the shelter and comfort of home to all who accept it.

DAY 99

BIBLE READING:

DEUTERONOMY 26:1–28:14; LUKE 10:1–20; PSALM 68:7–14

And the Lord shall make thee the head, and not the tail; and thou shalt be above only, and thou shalt not be beneath; if that thou hearken unto the commandments of the Lord thy God, which I command thee this day.
DEUTERONOMY 28:13

Many of God's Old Testament promises were conditional—*if* the people would do the right things, *then* God would bless them. Today though, in Jesus we receive God's blessing entirely apart from our own goodness (see Romans 5). We are truly "above only. . .not. . .beneath," and all because of God's kindness and love.

DAY 100

—— BIBLE READING: ——
DEUTERONOMY 28:15–68; LUKE 10:21–37;
PSALM 68:15–19

*And [Jesus] turned him unto his disciples,
and said privately, Blessed are the eyes
which see the things that ye see.*
LUKE 10:23

So many conundrums consume our days that we may wonder what it's like to be simply. . .happy. Jesus wants us to wonder no longer. He wants us to turn to Him in prayer (Matthew 21:22). He wants to carry our burdens (Matthew 11:29). He longs to have us lead lives that are built upon the life-giving foundation of His Word (John 6:63), and not on the shifting sands of popular thought.

DAY 101

── BIBLE READING: ──

DEUTERONOMY 29–30; LUKE 10:38–11:23; PSALM 68:20–27

If ye then, being evil, know how to give good gifts unto your children: how much more shall your heavenly Father give the Holy Spirit to them that ask him?

LUKE 11:13

What a beautiful reminder of the Lord's love for us, His children. While we—imperfect, sinful beings that we are—strive to give good things to our children, how does that compare to what God will give to us? Our God is perfect. Our God is sinless. Our God is love. Imagine what that means for us if we walk closely with Him. He will bless us beyond measure (Luke 11:28).

DAY 102

Be strong and of a good courage, fear not,
nor be afraid of them: for the LORD thy God,
he it is that doth go with thee; he will
not fail thee, nor forsake thee.
DEUTERONOMY 31:6

It's human nature to get wrapped up in relationships—spouses, friends, siblings, parents, and children. It's also human nature for people in these relationships to disappoint each other. But God promises His enduring faithfulness. His friendship will never disappoint.

DAY 103

— BIBLE READING: —

DEUTERONOMY 32:23–33:29; LUKE 11:37–54; PSALM 69:1–9

For their rock is not as our Rock.
DEUTERONOMY 32:31

Moses likened God to a Rock (notice the capital *R*) —strong, firm, and unchanging. Other religions might have "small-*r* rocks," but they just don't compare to ours. Why not? Because our Rock is the one and only Creator (Genesis 1:1), Sustainer (Romans 11:36), and Savior (Acts 4:11–12). Best of all, He knows everything about us and loves us just the same (Romans 5:8).

DAY 104

── BIBLE READING: ──

DEUTERONOMY 34–JOSHUA 2; LUKE 12:1-15; PSALM 69:10-17

Have not I commanded thee? Be strong and of a good courage; be not afraid, neither be thou dismayed: for the Lord thy God is with thee whithersoever thou goest.
JOSHUA 1:9

Read through today's scripture, and you're guaranteed to get a courage boost! What a lovely reminder that even when we are at our weakest, God is with us. It is through our weakness that God's power shines through (2 Corinthians 12:9). The next time you're struggling to get through a bad day, remember that God is right there, holding out His arms to you. He'll give you the comfort and strength you need.

DAY 105

For where your treasure is,
there will your heart be also.
LUKE 12:34

Jesus tells His followers to stop worrying about the details of their lives, to stop saving up earthly riches while ignoring Christ's kingdom. It takes a person with the foresight of heaven to realize the wealth, power, and material things of this world hold no everlasting importance. Jesus promises riches to the heart that makes deposits in heaven.

DAY 106

—— BIBLE READING: ——
JOSHUA 5:13–7:26; LUKE 12:41–48; PSALM 69:29–36

I will praise the name of God with a song,
and will magnify him with thanksgiving.
PSALM 69:30

Here's a promise that we, like the psalm writer, can make to the Lord. God loves music—especially when it praises His name. Have you heard a particular song you can sing to God today? Or is there one you can compose especially for Him? Give it a try—when you make God happy, you'll feel better yourself.

DAY 107

Thou art my help and my deliverer; O LORD.
PSALM 70:5

We all struggle with temptation in one form or another. And it's tough to stand strong all the time. We're only human after all. When our human weakness threatens to win out, call on the Lord. . .the only One who promises to provide us with a way out when the going gets tough (1 Corinthians 10:13).

DAY 108

*Then said he, Unto what is the kingdom of God
like? and whereunto shall I resemble it? It is like
a grain of mustard seed, which a man took,
and cast into his garden; and it grew,
and waxed a great tree; and the fowls
of the air lodged in the branches of it.*
LUKE 13:18–19

Although Jesus uses the idea of a tiny mustard seed
as a metaphor for faith, He also uses this word picture
to explain the kingdom of God. His followers may
have wondered if Jesus' influence would ever grow
beyond the small circle of His disciples. But the
Messiah promised God's holy nation will continue
to grow until it reaches full maturity.

DAY 109

───── BIBLE READING: ─────
JOSHUA 11:16–13:33; LUKE 13:22–35; PSALM 71:7–16

There are last which shall be first,
and there are first which shall be last.
LUKE 13:30

God never promised life would be fair. Money, good looks, and the right connections make life easy for some people. But that won't always be the case. Jesus' words give hope that a new day is coming, when the privileged few aren't always on top. If you're "last" now, take hope—through Jesus, you can be first!

DAY 110

Now therefore give me this mountain,
whereof the LORD spake in that day.
JOSHUA 14:12

Old Caleb was claiming a forty-five-year-old promise: as one of the two faithful spies who argued for taking the Promised Land, Caleb had received God's promise, through Moses, of a choice part of that land. Decades later, he cashed in. Though forty-five years may seem like a long time to us, it's barely a blip on God's eternal radar. Never doubt that He'll make good His promises to you too.

DAY 111

—— BIBLE READING: ——

JOSHUA 17:1–19:16; LUKE 14:16–35; PSALM 71:22–24

My lips shall greatly rejoice when I sing unto thee;
and my soul, which thou hast redeemed.
PSALM 71:23

Has your soul been set free? Or do you feel the weight of a heavy load on your heart? We are able to leave our cares at our Creator's feet (Psalm 55:22), and He promises to relieve us of any burdens we bear. Share your worries and concerns with Him, and feel the weight lift from your soul as it becomes freed from the cares of the world. Then praise God for the good things He has done for you (Isaiah 63:7).

DAY 112

*Likewise, I say unto you, there is joy in the presence
of the angels of God over one sinner that repenteth.*
LUKE 15:10

It's easy to rejoice when good things happen: a
goal achieved, an obstacle overcome, a project
completed. However, when we hear the good news
about a new Christian, the rejoicing isn't confined to
other believers only. The heavens erupt in beautiful
melody and happiness as the angels celebrate the new
reservation for one more soul in eternity with God.

DAY 113

And he said unto him, Son, thou art ever with me,
and all that I have is thine.
LUKE 15:31

Many know the story of the "prodigal son," the runaway who returned home to a loving father's welcome. Less familiar is the story's end, of the prodigal's responsible brother being angered by the father's generosity. The older man's comment, "All that I have is thine," is a picture of God's promise to us as His own heirs (Romans 8:17). Think about that—as Christians, we can enjoy everything God has and is!

DAY 114

And, behold, this day I am going the way of all the earth: and ye know in all your hearts and in all your souls, that not one thing hath failed of all the good things which the LORD your God spake concerning you; all are come to pass unto you, and not one thing hath failed thereof.
JOSHUA 23:14

If God says it, He'll do it. Who else in your life—your friends, your family, your neighbors, your coworkers—can you depend on quite like that? At one time or another, we've all been hurt because of a broken promise. What joy to know that there's One who will always make good on His word. Put your trust in Him today.

DAY 115

And the Lord said, If ye had faith as a grain of mustard seed, ye might say unto this sycamine tree, Be thou plucked up by the root, and be thou planted in the sea; and it should obey you.
LUKE 17:6

Jesus promises great power to His followers who display only a tiny amount of faith. Faith as small as a mustard seed, however, isn't the goal. Jesus' unspoken promise is that a Christian who displays faith as big as an apple seed or even a peach pit will be able to do more than move mountains. That kind of faith can change the world.

DAY 116

—— BIBLE READING: ——

JUDGES 3-4; LUKE 17:11-37; PSALM 73:21-28

And she said, I will surely go with thee:
notwithstanding the journey that thou
takest shall not be for thine honour;
for the LORD shall sell Sisera
into the hand of a woman.
JUDGES 4:9

We can learn a couple of lessons from this promise, spoken by one woman (Deborah) about another woman (Jael). First, God knows the future better than we know the present—because a humble housewife did indeed kill the mighty warrior Sisera. Second, though the stories of men tend to get more ink in the Bible, God also clearly loves and calls women to accomplish His plans for the world (see Galatians 3:28).

DAY 117

*But Jesus called them unto him, and said,
Suffer little children to come unto me, and forbid
them not: for of such is the kingdom of God.
Verily I say unto you, Whosoever shall
not receive the kingdom of God as a little
child shall in no wise enter therein.*
LUKE 18:16–17

In the passage above, Jesus is welcoming the little children. He doesn't see their innocence and wonder as an interruption or a nuisance. He reminds His disciples that there is something to be said for a childlike faith with His statement "for of such is the kingdom of God." We don't need to be Bible scholars or experts to inherit the kingdom of God; all we need is childlike faith—pure and simple.

DAY 118

——— BIBLE READING: ———

JUDGES 6:25-7:25; LUKE 18:18-43; PSALM 74:4-11

*And the LORD said unto Gideon, By the three
hundred men that lapped will I save you,
and deliver the Midianites into thine hand.*
JUDGES 7:7

What military commander would whittle his force
down from thirty-two thousand to three hundred?
That's exactly what Gideon did, at God's command.
God wanted a small force to fight the Midianites,
so the Israelites couldn't say their own strength had
achieved the victory. God promised a miracle, and
He delivered—when Gideon's tiny band, armed with
trumpets and lamps, shocked the sleeping enemy in
the dark of night. The Midianites, terrified by the light
and sound, attacked each other before other Israelites
mopped up the survivors.

DAY 119

BIBLE READING:

JUDGES 8:1–9:23; LUKE 19:1–28; PSALM 74:12–17

*For the Son of man is come to seek
and to save that which was lost.*
LUKE 19:10

Which is the best promise in the whole Bible? It might be this one. Jesus came looking for *you*, in the hope of saving you from the punishment of sin. And He's perfectly able to do that—you just have to take hold of the free gift of salvation (see Romans 3:24). If you haven't taken advantage of this amazing offer, why not do so now?

DAY 120

And [Jesus] answered and said unto them,
I tell you that, if these should hold their peace,
the stones would immediately cry out.
LUKE 19:40

Have you heard the expression "Dumb as a box of rocks"? Jesus said that if people didn't praise Him, then the rest of His creation—including stones—would. That's a promise we shouldn't hope to see fulfilled. Don't be dumb—praise the Lord today!

DAY 121

*The earth and all the inhabitants thereof are
dissolved: I bear up the pillars of it. Selah.*
PSALM 75:3

God promises to hold the world and its people together when times are unstable. Imagine the entire
earth shaking—creating fear and unease among the
people. Now imagine God's hands wrapped around
the world, holding it steady—and the people sighing
with utter relief. That's what God does. He makes it
possible for us to have calm in a world that is often
filled with chaos and instability.

DAY 122

For he is not a God of the dead,
but of the living: for all live unto him.
Luke 20:38

If some people are guilty of putting God in a box, others are guilty of putting Him in heaven and leaving Him there. God isn't simply sitting on a cloud twiddling His thumbs, waiting for His children to approach the pearly gates. Jesus reminds His followers that His Father is the God of the living. In earthly life and in physical death, He's real and living and vibrant.

DAY 123

BIBLE READING:

JUDGES 15-16; LUKE 21:1-19; PSALM 76:1-7

But before all these, they shall lay their hands on you, and persecute you, delivering you up to the synagogues, and into prisons, being brought before kings and rulers for my name's sake.
LUKE 21:12

Jesus never painted a rosy picture of the Christian life. Hard work, family tensions, and outright persecution might be in line for us, just as they were for the original disciples. But remember this life is short— and, as the apostle Paul promised, "I reckon that the sufferings of this present time are not worthy to be compared with the glory which shall be revealed in us" (Romans 8:18).

DAY 124

———— BIBLE READING: ————

JUDGES 17–18; LUKE 21:20–22:6; PSALM 76:8–12

And when these things begin to come to pass,
then look up, and lift up your heads;
for your redemption draweth nigh.
LUKE 21:28

"These things" refers to events that will take place before the return of Christ (see verses 20–27). Terrible things will come to pass. People will fear for their lives; they will be tempted to give up. But the Lord promises that because we have been bought with His blood, we can lift up our heads. Our days of freedom will come—an eternity spent with Him in paradise.

DAY 125

I cried unto God with my voice, even unto God with my voice; and he gave ear unto me.
PSALM 77:1

Calling toll-free numbers to most large businesses almost always guarantees the voice on the other end will be an automated service. Making your way through a maze of phone options to a real human is usually frustrating and sometimes impossible. God's hotline guarantees no preprogrammed voice messages. A prayer spoken calmly with hands clasped, or shouted in the middle of a storm, doesn't go unheard. God hears and listens.

DAY 126

*Thou hast with thine arm redeemed thy people,
the sons of Jacob and Joseph. Selah.*
PSALM 77:15

This verse tells of God's miraculous deliverance of
the ancient Israelites from their slavery in Egypt. But
God is still in the business of setting people free today.
Here's a promise worth memorizing, and revisiting
day after day: "I am the way, the truth, and the life"
(John 14:6); "ye shall know the truth, and the truth
shall make you free" (John 8:32).

DAY 127

—— BIBLE READING: ——
RUTH 1–2; LUKE 22:55–23:25; PSALM 78:1–4

The LORD recompense thy work, and a full reward be given thee of the LORD God of Israel, under whose wings thou art come to trust.
RUTH 2:12

Sing praises to God today for His protection and His strength. In the midst of the storm, He offers us peace (John 14:27). He gives us shelter. He calms our fearful hearts. He wraps us in His love. Nowhere else can we find such comfort. When lightning strikes and winds blow fierce, call out to Him.

DAY 128

And as they were afraid, and bowed down their faces to the earth, they said unto them, Why seek ye the living among the dead? He is not here, but is risen: remember how he spake unto you when he was yet in Galilee, saying, The Son of man must be delivered into the hands of sinful men, and be crucified, and the third day rise again.
LUKE 24:5–7

As God's children wait for His promises of heaven and everlasting life to be fulfilled, it's comforting to experience promises that have already been fulfilled. Jesus' biggest promise ever—that He'd rise from the dead—was fulfilled in a mere three days, just as He said it would be.

DAY 129

And she vowed a vow, and said, O LORD of hosts,
if thou wilt indeed look on the affliction of thine
handmaid, and remember me, and not forget
thine handmaid, but wilt give unto thine
handmaid a man child, then I will give
him unto the LORD all the days of his life.
1 SAMUEL 1:11

A desperate, childless woman begs for a son, promising to give the boy back in service to God. The Lord blesses Hannah with a son named Samuel, who becomes one of Israel's greatest leaders—but only because Hannah kept her word. As the writer of Ecclesiastes reminds us, "When thou vowest a vow unto God, defer not to pay it; for he hath no pleasure in fools: pay that which thou hast vowed" (Ecclesiastes 5:4).

DAY 130

1 SAMUEL 2:22–4:22; JOHN 1:1–28; PSALM 78:17–24

*Wherefore the L*ORD *God of Israel saith. . .
them that honour me I will honour.*
1 SAMUEL 2:30

Although God was speaking to the high priest Eli concerning his disobedient sons, God's promise applies to us too. "I love them that love me," God says in Proverbs 8:17, "and those that seek me early shall find me." Don't wait another day to honor God; open His Book and spend some time talking to Him. He loves to hear from you!

DAY 131

───── BIBLE READING: ─────

1 SAMUEL 5–7; JOHN 1:29–51; PSALM 78:25–33

And Samuel spake unto all the house of Israel, saying, If ye do return unto the LORD with all your hearts, then put away the strange gods and Ashtaroth from among you, and prepare your hearts unto the LORD, and serve him only: and he will deliver you out of the hand of the Philistines.
1 SAMUEL 7:3

While we might not need to be saved from the Philistines, this verse is a good reminder that when we place our faith and trust entirely in the Lord, He can—and will—do amazing things in our lives. He will reward those who seek Him with their whole hearts (Hebrews 11:1, 6). Step out in faith and be blessed beyond measure today!

DAY 132

Jesus answered and said unto them, Destroy this temple, and in three days I will raise it up.
JOHN 2:19

It took more than a lifetime of work for Jesus to change the views held by the religious leaders of His day. His promise was that when His physical body was killed, He'd rise again in three days. The religious leaders of Jesus' time were so focused on the symbolic importance of the actual temple, they completely missed the importance of the temple of God and the house for His Spirit, Christ's body.

DAY 133

—— BIBLE READING: ——
1 SAMUEL 9:27–11:15; JOHN 3:1–22; PSALM 78:42–55

*Jesus answered and said unto him, Verily, verily,
I say unto thee, Except a man be born again,
he cannot see the kingdom of God.*
JOHN 3:3

Ever hear a kid ask, "Is that a promise or a threat?"
These words of Jesus are a bit of both. By being
born again, people enter God's kingdom. But there's
no entry apart from the free gift of salvation—no
amount of kindness, hard work, or charitable giving
will punch your ticket to heaven. For more on being
"born again," read on to verse 16.

DAY 134

Moreover as for me, God forbid that I should sin against the LORD in ceasing to pray for you: but I will teach you the good and the right way.
1 SAMUEL 12:23

Near the end of his life, the prophet Samuel promised the Israelites that he would teach them "the good and the right way." Verse 24 explains what that good and right way is: "Fear the LORD, and serve him in truth with all your heart. . .consider how great things he hath done for you." What was good for the ancient Israelites is just as good for us today.

DAY 135

But whosoever drinketh of the water that I shall give him shall never thirst; but the water that I shall give him shall be in him a well of water springing up into everlasting life.
JOHN 4:14

The dry, burning sensation of thirst is one that most humans can easily remedy. The wet refreshment of a tall glass of crystal-clear water sends the most desperate of thirsts away. But it always comes back. Jesus uses an eternal thirst-quenching water as a metaphor for the hope, peace, and satisfaction God offers His children who enter into a relationship with Him. It's water that no amount of Satan-salt can overpower.

DAY 136

And Samuel said, Hath the LORD as great delight in burnt offerings and sacrifices, as in obeying the voice of the LORD? Behold, to obey is better than sacrifice, and to hearken than the fat of rams.
1 SAMUEL 15:22

Get your arms around this Bible promise, and life will run much smoother! God wants us to obey the rules He's set up to protect us and to help us grow. He's far less interested in our "paying back" in some way after we've done wrong. What could we ever pay God anyway? "If a man love me," Jesus said, "he will keep my words" (John 14:23).

DAY 137

*Verily, verily, I say unto you, He that heareth
my word, and believeth on him that sent me,
hath everlasting life, and shall not come into
condemnation; but is passed from death unto life.*
JOHN 5:24

While it's normal to mourn the passing of loved
ones—fellow believers in Christ—isn't it wonderful
that we can, at the same time, celebrate their much-
anticipated entrance into the presence of God? For
those who have trusted in the Lord as their Savior,
death isn't the end of life; it's just the beginning of
eternity.

DAY 138

*Turn us again, O God of hosts, and cause
thy face to shine; and we shall be saved.*
PSALM 80:7

A person who saves the life of another is often heralded as a hero. Acts of selflessness, moments of impulse, and good deeds can result in heroes. But God's heroic deed of saving His people is a sacrifice He thoughtfully and consciously made. The heavenly Father gave up His only Son for humankind. His powerful grace can save the low and the mighty.

DAY 139

And Jonathan said to David, Go in peace, forasmuch as we have sworn both of us in the name of the Lord, saying, The Lord be between me and thee, and between my seed and thy seed for ever.
1 Samuel 20:42

This promise sealed one of the greatest friendships of all time. King Saul's son Jonathan, next in line for the throne, pledged his love and support for his friend David, chosen by God to be Israel's next ruler. What a picture of Paul's command to "in lowliness of mind let each esteem other better than themselves" (Philippians 2:3)!

DAY 140

*Jesus answered them and said, Verily, verily,
I say unto you, Ye seek me, not because ye
saw the miracles, but because ye did
eat of the loaves, and were filled.*
JOHN 6:26

Their physical hunger was only satisfied for a time, and the people went searching for more. Yet Jesus knew their needs went much deeper. Only when we develop a personal relationship with Jesus, and acknowledge Him as Lord and Savior, do we feel truly "filled." Then we can celebrate the promise along with the psalmist: "O taste and see that the LORD is good" (Psalm 34:8).

DAY 141

——— BIBLE READING: ———
1 SAMUEL 24:1–25:31; JOHN 6:43–71; PSALM 81:11–16

*Oh that my people had hearkened unto me,
and Israel had walked in my ways! I should
soon have subdued their enemies, and turned
my hand against their adversaries.*
PSALM 81:13–14

Do you ever long for strength and courage in the face
of your enemies? Look to this promise when you're
feeling weak and helpless. The Lord offers His power
to help us defeat those who rise against us—if only
we listen to Him and obey Him. He will never leave
us to fight our battles alone (Hebrews 13:5–6).

DAY 142

Arise, O God, judge the earth:
for thou shalt inherit all nations.
PSALM 82:8

National borders, cultural differences, and racial friction are just a few of the issues that plague humankind's desire for unity. Finding common ground is often difficult if not impossible. No matter how vast the canyon between the nations of the world, the truth is that God is the Creator of all. His children can find unity in Him.

DAY 143

*Jesus stood and cried, saying, If any man thirst,
let him come unto me, and drink.*
JOHN 7:37

What's better than a cool glass of water on a hot, dry day? Jesus paints that picture of Himself, promising spiritual refreshment to anyone who turns to Him in faith. The thirsty soul and others around benefit, for "he that believeth on me, as the scripture hath said, out of his belly shall flow rivers of living water" (John 7:38). Don't you want to be refreshed? Don't you want to be a refresher?

DAY 144

Blessed are they that dwell in thy house:
they will be still praising thee. Selah.
PSALM 84:4

Some Christians radiate joy wherever they go. They can't help but pass their happiness on to others—through a smile, a kind word, a helping hand. As a child of God, this same kind of joy belongs to you too. Let your heart fill with joy (Psalm 28:7), but don't keep it to yourself. Pass it on!

DAY 145

*Jesus said unto them, Verily, verily,
I say unto you, Before Abraham was, I am.*
JOHN 8:58

Christians tend to think of eternity in terms of the future: heaven will be the eternal home for God's children. Eternity, however, stretches not only into the future but into the past as well. Jesus told His followers that He was and is and always will be. Christ promises His children this everlasting comfort of His presence.

DAY 146

——— BIBLE READING: ———
2 SAMUEL 3–4; JOHN 9:13–34; PSALM 85:1–7

*Thou hast forgiven the iniquity of thy people,
thou hast covered all their sin. Selah.*
PSALM 85:2

Living as we do in the "Christian era," we can read Psalm 85:2 in light of Jesus' perfect sacrifice. His death on the cross covered every sin, paving the way for the forgiveness of everyone who asks. God takes His promise of forgiveness *very* seriously—it cost Him the death of His Son!

DAY 147

2 SAMUEL 5:1–7:17; JOHN 9:35–10:10; PSALM 85:8–13

Yea, the LORD shall give that which is good;
and our land shall yield her increase.
PSALM 85:12

We've all heard the saying "Good things come to those who wait." But let's improve upon that statement with "Good things come to those who put their trust in the Lord." It's not about waiting it out—something good eventually has to happen to us, right? But it is about loving the Lord and trusting Him to give us exactly what we need.

DAY 148

And I give unto [my sheep] eternal life;
and they shall never perish, neither shall
any man pluck them out of my hand.
JOHN 10:28

Jesus' followers would have been very familiar with the relationship between a shepherd and his sheep. As a shepherd cares for his flock and looks out for its well-being, so much more does Jesus value each of His followers. Jesus is the ultimate Shepherd as He extends eternal life, freedom from punishment, and safety in His hand.

DAY 149

*When Jesus heard that, he said, This sickness
is not unto death, but for the glory of God,
that the Son of God might be glorified thereby.*
JOHN 11:4

Nobody asks for illness or injury. But God has
promised that even our worst experiences can serve
His good purposes. Remember Romans 8:28? "And
we know that all things work together for good to
them that love God, to them who are the called
according to his purpose." Having a tough day (or
week, or year, or life)? You can still bring honor
to God.

DAY 150

*Jesus said unto her, I am the resurrection,
and the life: he that believeth in me,
though he were dead, yet shall he live.*
JOHN 11:25

Martha's brother, Lazarus, had been in his tomb for four days when Jesus arrived to speak these words. Why had Jesus waited so long to come to the aid of His dear friend? The answer is clear: to demonstrate in no uncertain terms that He is God. The One who gives life can be no other than the One who created the heavens and the earth from nothing (see Genesis 1:1).

DAY 151

Let my prayer come before thee:
incline thine ear unto my cry.
PSALM 88:2

Although the Lord may not seem to hear us when we call out to Him, we must persevere. Luke 18:1 reminds us that we should pray and never give up. Just because we haven't received an answer doesn't mean we should quit praying about a particular matter; it simply means we should keep praying, with faith in our hearts, that the Lord will come through—at just the right time.

DAY 152

——— BIBLE READING: ———

2 SAMUEL 15:13-16:23; JOHN 12:20-43; PSALM 88:10-18

*If any man serve me, let him follow me; and where
I am, there shall also my servant be: if any man
serve me, him will my Father honour.*
JOHN 12:26

It isn't often that we hear the word *honor* uttered
in a sentence. When we do, the term seems rather
outdated—a thing of the past. But Jesus says if we
serve Him, His Father will honor us. He will treat
us with high regard. While the people we live and
work among may not accept our service to the Lord
with open hearts and minds, we need to look at the
bigger picture and relish the thought that our Father
in heaven will reward us for our endeavors. And
that's all that really matters anyway.

DAY 153

—— BIBLE READING: ——

2 SAMUEL 17:1–18:18; JOHN 12:44–13:20; PSALM 89:1–6

I am come a light into the world, that whosoever believeth on me should not abide in darkness.
JOHN 12:46

Fear of darkness is one of those childhood phobias that sometimes sticks around to adulthood. Why? Because we can't see in the dark. Darkness can lead to uncertainty, confusion, and even paranoia. Evil creatures lurk in the dark. Secrets hide in the dark. Jesus offered an alternative to the darkness and evil of the world when He promised to illuminate the lives of His children who trust in Him.

DAY 154

BIBLE READING:
2 SAMUEL 18:19–19:39; JOHN 13:21–38; PSALM 89:7–13

O LORD God of hosts, who is a strong LORD like unto thee? or to thy faithfulness round about thee?
PSALM 89:8

The word *faithful* can be defined as "firm in adherence to promises." And that describes God exactly. Through almost half a year now, you've read promises from scripture and seen how the Lord has fulfilled every one. Say today with the psalm writer, "All around You we see how faithful You are!"

DAY 155

Jesus saith unto him, I am the way, the truth, and the life: no man cometh unto the Father, but by me.
JOHN 14:6

Good works won't get you there. Being nice won't get you there. Success won't get you there. Lots of money won't get you there. The only way there—to eternal life in heaven with our Creator—is through Jesus (Ephesians 2:8–9). If we believe in Him and accept His gift of salvation, we will one day live in a state of perfect peace and joy in a place prepared especially for us, His children (John 14:2–3).

DAY 156

BIBLE READING:
2 SAMUEL 22:1–23:7; JOHN 14:18–15:27;
PSALM 89:19–29

*But the Comforter, which is the Holy Ghost,
whom the Father will send in my name, he shall
teach you all things, and bring all things to your
remembrance, whatsoever I have said unto you.*
JOHN 14:26

When Jesus took up residence with His Father in heaven, His followers may have felt ill-equipped to continue growing His kingdom on earth. Thankfully, the Messiah didn't leave them empty handed. He extends that same help to every Christian: the Holy Spirit, who fills in the gaps when head knowledge fails.

DAY 157

Ye shall be sorrowful,
but your sorrow shall be turned into joy.
JOHN 16:20

Jesus made this promise to His disciples as He described his impending death and resurrection. But the idea of Jesus' words applies to us today: We have sorrow and trouble in this world (John 16:33), but look forward to a day when every tear will be wiped away by God Himself (Revelation 7:17). No matter how hard this world may be, a better day is coming!

DAY 158

*Then Adonijah the son of Haggith
exalted himself, saying, I will be king.*
1 KINGS 1:5

Adonijah, a son of King David, promised himself and his followers that he would follow his father on the throne. But David had said his younger son Solomon would be king—so Adonijah's words proved empty. Some "promises" are beyond our ability to keep, and shouldn't even be made. "There are many devices in a man's heart; nevertheless the counsel of the LORD, that shall stand" (Proverbs 19:21).

DAY 159

*Holy Father, keep through thine own
name those whom thou hast given me,
that they may be one, as we are.*
JOHN 17:11

Jesus prayed this prayer just before the arrest that
led to His crucifixion. Even while He was anticipating
the horrible pain that awaited Him in the coming
hours, the Messiah spent time praying for Christians.
He promises unity among believers who tap into the
power of the name of God.

DAY 160

*That the saying might be fulfilled, which he spake,
Of them which thou gavest me have I lost none.*
JOHN 18:9

When we come to God through Jesus, we're secure.
God has wrapped His protective wings around us
(Psalm 63:7), He is a Strong Tower for us (Proverbs 18:10), and He cares for us (1 Peter 5:7).
Jesus has said that nobody will snatch us from His
hands (John 10:28). Come to God through Jesus,
and He'll never let you go.

DAY 161

— BIBLE READING: —
1 KINGS 5–6; JOHN 18:28–19:5; PSALM 91:1–10

And the LORD gave Solomon wisdom,
as he promised him.
1 KINGS 5:12

Solomon once wrote, "How much better is it to get wisdom than gold!" (Proverbs 16:16), but as one who abused that gift, he also knew the flip side of such power (Ecclesiastes 1:18). Far better, then, to be filled, as Paul writes, "with the knowledge of his will in all wisdom and spiritual understanding" (Colossians 1:9). When we seek God's will and wisdom, we can live lives that are "worthy of the Lord unto all pleasing" (Colossians 1:10).

DAY 162

BIBLE READING:
1 KINGS 7; JOHN 19:6-24; PSALM 91:11-16

*For he shall give his angels charge over thee,
to keep thee in all thy ways.*
PSALM 91:11

No need for armed bodyguards. No need to let fear overtake us. No need to cower in the face of our enemies. God is our Protector. His strength and power will keep us from harm. His shelter is enough to keep us safe. If we place our hope and trust in Him, He'll even command His angels to care for us. Nowhere else but God's Word can you find a promise like that.

DAY 163

After this, Jesus knowing that all things were now accomplished, that the scripture might be fulfilled.
JOHN 19:28

Jesus Christ fulfilled more than three hundred Old Testament prophesies about the Messiah. From the ministry of John the Baptist (Isaiah 40:3) and Jesus' birth in Bethlehem (Micah 5:2), to His betrayal by a friend (Psalm 41:9) and the piercing of His hands and feet (Psalm 22:16), Jesus' life had been spelled out in prophecy generations before He stepped foot on earth. He is truly a promise fulfilled.

DAY 164

──── BIBLE READING: ────

1 KINGS 8:54–10:13; JOHN 20:1-18; PSALM 92:10-15

*To shew that the L*ORD *is upright: he is my rock,*
and there is no unrighteousness in him.
PSALM 92:15

Bottom line: you can trust God. He is faithful. He's a Rock. He's absolutely right and good in every way. Even when you're going through hard times. Even when life isn't making sense. Even when God seems distant. Think about all the fulfilled promises you've read about through the first five and a half months of this year—and recommit yourself to the good and faithful God who loves you!

DAY 165

Jesus saith unto him, Thomas, because thou hast seen me, thou hast believed: blessed are they that have not seen, and yet have believed.
JOHN 20:29

Are you a Doubting Thomas? Do you need to see something in order to believe it? Or are you a Believing Benjamin—believing without needing visual evidence? The Lord wants us to have faith in His promises without a need for signs or proof to back them up. If we have faith—placing our trust in His Word—He promises our happiness, pure and simple.

DAY 166

——— BIBLE READING: ———
1 KINGS 12:1–13:10; JOHN 21; PSALM 94:1–11

The LORD knoweth the thoughts of man,
that they are vanity.
PSALM 94:11

Sometimes it's difficult to get past daily stresses to see what's really important. When everything seems hopeless, helpless, and out of control, God still sees the big picture. His children can take comfort in the fact that God knows all and sees all. And His shoulders are strong enough to bear the stresses and frustrations of the day.

DAY 167

BIBLE READING:

1 KINGS 13:11–14:31; ACTS 1:1–11; PSALM 94:12–23

But ye shall receive power, after that the Holy Ghost is come upon you: and ye shall be witnesses unto me both in Jerusalem, and in all Judaea, and in Samaria, and unto the uttermost part of the earth.

ACTS 1:8

Though the resurrected Jesus had to leave earth for heaven, He promised to send His Holy Spirit to His followers. And what a powerful presence the Spirit is! Read the book of Acts to see what the Spirit helped the early Christians do. Read Galatians 5:22–23 to see what He'll help you to achieve. Don't miss out on this promise!

DAY 168

*In his hand are the deep places of the earth:
the strength of the hills is his also. The sea is his,
and he made it: and his hands formed the dry land.*
PSALM 95:4–5

Take a good look at all our Creator has provided for our enjoyment—the mountains, the sea, the sky, the flowers and trees. All these beautiful things were created with us in mind. . .and all belong to Him. Thank the Lord today for His goodness and for the simple pleasures He has placed in your backyard.

DAY 169

For all the gods of the nations are idols: but the LORD made the heavens. Honour and majesty are before him: strength and beauty are in his sanctuary.
PSALM 96:5–6

Fans of professional athletes and teams often find themselves defending the greatness of their heroes. It's a "my dad is stronger than your dad" kind of argument that will never really be resolved. Children of God sometimes find themselves defending their Father to a world that thinks truth is relative. But all other gods—wealth, power, possessions—are empty, and only the true Creator can claim great power.

DAY 170

BIBLE READING:

1 KINGS 18:20–19:21; ACTS 2:22–41; PSALM 96:9–13

*Yet I have left me seven thousand in Israel,
all the knees which have not bowed unto Baal,
and every mouth which hath not kissed him.*
1 KINGS 19:18

Poor Elijah was depressed. Soon after destroying the prophets of Baal at Carmel, he heard Queen Jezebel's threat to snuff out *his* life—and, thinking he was the only true prophet left, Elijah lost heart. But God promised to keep a small army of faithful people in Israel—just as He keeps His program alive today. Sure, you're living in a dark, scary world. But remember that He'll never leave you alone (see Matthew 19:29).

DAY 171

Clouds and darkness are round about him:
righteousness and judgment are the
habitation of his throne.
PSALM 97:2

When you quarrel with your spouse, your kids won't listen to you, and your boss is on the verge of handing you a pink slip, there's a tendency to blame God for your misfortune. Still, we need to remember that our heavenly Father is always just. He causes His sun to rise over all people. . .and His rain to pour down as well (Matthew 5:45).

DAY 172

BIBLE READING:

1 KINGS 21:1–22:28; ACTS 4:1–22; PSALM 97:7–12

*Ye that love the LORD, hate evil: he preserveth
the souls of his saints; he delivereth them
out of the hand of the wicked.*
PSALM 97:10

Perfect peace is the gift we will receive if we remain faithful to our Father God (John 14:27). With Him as our closest companion, we can weather any storm. The world may toss some scary things our way, but we can stand untouched with God as our Shield. In the words of Jesus, "These things I have spoken unto you, that in me ye might have peace. In the world ye shall have tribulation: but be of good cheer; I have overcome the world" (John 16:33).

DAY 173

1 KINGS 22:29–2 KINGS 1; ACTS 4:23–5:11; PSALM 98

*All the ends of the earth have seen
the salvation of our God.*
PSALM 98:3

An open eye and a listening ear can see and hear God's graces on a daily basis: a helping hand from a coworker on the busiest of days; a series of green traffic lights to get to an appointment on time. That same sensitivity to God can see His saving power on a grander scale: a hurricane heading straight for land veers out to sea; a biopsy expected to indicate cancer comes back cancer-free. Everyone everywhere has experienced this saving power. It's up to His children to help others see it.

DAY 174

And Elisha said unto him, As the LORD liveth,
and as thy soul liveth, I will not leave thee.
2 KINGS 2:2

This promise is loyalty on display: Elisha, successor
to the prophet Elijah, refused to leave his mentor's
side until God Himself swept Elijah up to heaven in
a chariot of fire. How much better would our world
be if everyone kept promises as well as Elisha did?

DAY 175

BIBLE READING:
2 KINGS 4; ACTS 5:29–6:15; PSALM 100

For the L<small>ORD</small> is good; his mercy is everlasting;
and his truth endureth to all generations.
P<small>SALM</small> 100:5

You can leave material goods. . . . You can leave money. . . . You can leave a name. . . . But the lovingkindness of the Lord. . .what a legacy to hand down to our children. And He promises just that for our children to come. We can leave a lasting inheritance for future generations—one that won't rust or fade over time. One that will never be depleted—because the Lord has promised it will last forever.

DAY 176

I will sing of mercy and judgment:
unto thee, O LORD, will I sing.
PSALM 101:1

We learn at an early age that life isn't always fair. At work, the immoral succeed and the cheaters get the promotion. In the court system, criminals go free and victims suffer again and again. But God doesn't play by the rules of the world. His righteous fairness transcends the imperfection of the world. He's truly worthy of our praise!

DAY 177

And he said, Behold, thou shalt see it with thine eyes, but shalt not eat thereof.
2 KINGS 7:2

Samaria was under military siege—and starving. When the prophet Elisha told the city's leaders that God was about to end the famine, one military captain doubted. Elisha's response was a frightening promise—proven true the next day when crowds rushing for a miraculous food supply trampled the captain to death. The point? Never doubt God's Word or abilities. Take what He offers with gratitude.

DAY 178

BIBLE READING:

2 KINGS 8:16–9:37; ACTS 7:37–53; PSALM 102:8–17

He will regard the prayer of the destitute,
and not despise their prayer.
PSALM 102:17

When you're in need, sometimes you feel utterly helpless and alone. Your closest friends may desert you. Your family may fail to give you support and help when you need it most. But there is One who will never turn His back on you. Draw near to Him and share your deepest needs and hurts with Him. You'll be glad you did.

DAY 179

—— BIBLE READING: ——
2 KINGS 10-11; ACTS 7:54-8:8; PSALM 102:18-28

But thou art the same,
and thy years shall have no end.
PSALM 102:27

High school reunions bring their fair share of jitters to many classmates who haven't seen each other in years. Who has changed the most? Who looks the same? Who is the unexpected success story, and who is falling short of his or her potential? God is different from long-lost classmates. No matter how long one of God's children strays from a relationship with Him, the Father will be the same loving, powerful Creator that He has been forever.

DAY 180

The Lord is merciful and gracious,
slow to anger, and plenteous in mercy.
PSALM 103:8

How much "loving-pity and kindness" does God have toward us? Enough to send His only Son, Jesus, to die on the cross for us—even while we were still sinners (Romans 5:8). Enough to show patience to all people, not wanting anyone to miss the blessings of heaven (2 Peter 3:9). Enough to fulfill every promise He makes to us.

DAY 181

But the Lord said unto him, Go thy way: for he is a chosen vessel unto me, to bear my name before the Gentiles, and kings, and the children of Israel.
Acts 9:15

When the Lord gave this order to Ananias, the godly man was naturally skeptical. How could God have chosen Saul of Tarsus, a known killer of Christians, to be His missionary? Yet the man who would be called Paul became one of the most zealous evangelists of all time. How does God choose anyone? Let's remember God's promise to Samuel: "The Lord looketh on the heart" (1 Samuel 16:7).

DAY 182

The LORD hath prepared his throne in the heavens; and his kingdom ruleth over all.
PSALM 103:19

Presidents. . .senators. . .civic officials. . . No matter who they are or what the issue, our leaders have drastically different viewpoints. Sometimes they make bad decisions. No matter who holds an office, we're sure to be disappointed in a leader at some point. What a joy to know that while our earthly rulers may fail, we can always rely on our King in heaven to retain complete control over all.

DAY 183

[God,] who coverest thyself with light as with a garment: who stretchest out the heavens like a curtain: who layeth the beams of his chambers in the waters: who maketh the clouds his chariot: who walketh upon the wings of the wind: Who maketh his angels spirits; his ministers a flaming fire.
PSALM 104:2–4

God is in control. It's a simple fact, but in it are wrapped details that are easy to overlook. He controls all aspects of the world, from light and clouds to water and wind. His influence spreads over everything humans understand and everything beyond our grasp. He's in charge, and that's something we can rely on.

DAY 184

2 KINGS 19:8–20:21; ACTS 10:17–33; PSALM 104:10–23

*Now therefore are we all here present before God,
to hear all things that are commanded thee of God.*
ACTS 10:33

When the Roman soldier Cornelius made this promise
to the apostle Peter, God revealed that His plan of
salvation was for *everyone*—not only Jews. Cornelius
and his family believed in Jesus and received the
Holy Spirit, and the world has never been the same.
Just think how your own life might change if you
sincerely repeated the promise of Cornelius.

DAY 185

2 KINGS 21:1–22:20; ACTS 10:34–11:18; PSALM 104:24–30

*Whosoever believeth in him shall
receive remission of sins.*
Acts 10:43

Guilt. We've all experienced it at some point in our lives. A "little white lie" here. A bit of gossip passed along there. That really big, super-duper sin we've kept hidden from everyone. You get the picture. While others may not be aware of our shortcomings, God knows about them all. We can't keep anything from Him. The good news is that all we need to do is ask Him for forgiveness, and it's done—immediately, right then and there (1 John 1:9).

DAY 186

He looketh on the earth, and it trembleth:
he toucheth the hills, and they smoke.
PSALM 104:32

God is love, but God is also mighty power. The same God who extends grace to all who accept it also holds the power to destroy those who anger Him. For a Christian, the Creator's power can be a source of comfort as well as fear. It's only through the soul-cleansing blood of Christ that Christians can be confident in the fact that God's power is there to provide protection.

DAY 187

And the LORD sent against him bands of the
Chaldees, and bands of the Syrians, and bands
of the Moabites, and bands of the children
of Ammon, and sent them against Judah to
destroy it, according to the word of the LORD,
which he spake by his servants the prophets.
2 KINGS 24:2

Some of the Bible's promises aren't pleasant—they're warnings of punishment and destruction and pain. But notice how often God provides an "out" from His anger. All through the Old Testament, He said things like, "If you obey, you'll be safe." In the New Testament, God offers Jesus Christ as our escape from punishment and pain. Have you grabbed hold of that promise in John 3:16?

DAY 188

He hath remembered his covenant for ever; the word which he commanded to a thousand generations.
PSALM 105:8

Have you ever made a promise and soon forgot about it? "I promise I'll call you tonight at 7:00." "I promise I'll be there!" "I promise I'll. . ." We don't always place a lot of value on the promises we make to others, but there is One who stays true to His word—no matter how big or small the promise. Praise Him today.

DAY 189

For so hath the Lord commanded us, saying,
I have set thee to be a light of the Gentiles,
that thou shouldest be for salvation
unto the ends of the earth.
Acts 13:47

Paul and Barnabas are quoting a passage from Isaiah 49, explaining to Jewish leaders that the Word of God is extended to every person, regardless of race, family lineage, social status, or location. This promise reaches to the twenty-first century, as Christians are commanded in the Great Commission to share this promise of salvation from punishment with the entire world.

DAY 190

*Confirming the souls of the disciples, and
exhorting them to continue in the faith,
and that we must through much tribulation
enter into the kingdom of God.*
ACTS 14:22

Oh no. . .another promise of trials in the Christian life!
This time, the apostle Paul makes the promise, and he
knows what he's saying: just three verses earlier, he was
stoned and left for dead by an angry mob in Lycaonia.
Though it may not seem fair, God says we'll sometimes
suffer for following Him. But He also promises blessing
amid the pain (see Matthew 5:11–12).

DAY 191

*Known unto God are all his works from
the beginning of the world.*
ACTS 15:18

From the first words of the Old Testament—that God created heaven and earth—to the last—that Jesus will someday come to earth again—God has mapped out His plan for the world. And while we don't know the exact day or time of His return (Matthew 24:36), we can put our faith in the One called Alpha and Omega (Revelation 22:13), the First and the Last, and in His promises.

DAY 192

BIBLE READING:
1 CHRONICLES 9:10–11:9; ACTS 15:19–41; PSALM 106:1–12

*Praise ye the LORD. O give thanks unto the LORD;
for he is good: for his mercy endureth for ever.*
PSALM 106:1

Perfect weather on your day off. A warm house on a cold day. A much-needed hug from a friend. A pay increase at just the right time. It's not often that we stop and take notice of the little things the Lord has done for us. But each day, you're sure to find one thing to be thankful for. What will you praise Him for today?

DAY 193

BIBLE READING:
1 CHRONICLES 11:10-12:40; ACTS 16:1-15;
PSALM 106:13-27

For at that time day by day there came to David to help him, until it was a great host, like the host of God.
1 CHRONICLES 12:22

During times of war, we hear news about troop deployment and reinforcement, phrases that sometimes give the idea that our side isn't exactly winning. God's army isn't like human armies; His troop levels are big enough to conquer any enemy—even Satan himself.

DAY 194

—— BIBLE READING: ——
1 CHRONICLES 13–15; ACTS 16:16–40; PSALM 106:28–33

And they said, Believe on the Lord Jesus Christ,
and thou shalt be saved, and thy house.
ACTS 16:31

These seventeen words encapsulate the message of the entire Bible. In eternity past, long before Adam and Eve's sin in the Garden of Eden, God had planned a way to save people from punishment (Ephesians 1:3–5). In eternity future, we'll enjoy the pleasures and benefits of heaven (Psalm 16:11). And it's all through our faith in Jesus Christ.

DAY 195

Seek the LORD and his strength,
seek his face continually.
1 CHRONICLES 16:11

What do you do to rejuvenate when you're feeling weak? Take a long nap? Devour a home-cooked meal? Take a brisk walk? What about asking the Lord to give you strength? He alone has just the grace we need during our weakest moments (2 Corinthians 12:9). Ask Him to infuse you with His power. You won't regret it!

DAY 196

God that made the world and all things therein,
seeing that he is Lord of heaven and earth,
dwelleth not in temples made with hands;
neither is worshipped with men's hands, as
though he needed any thing, seeing he giveth
to all life, and breath, and all things.
ACTS 17:24–25

Evidence of god and goddess worship pervaded every aspect of life in first-century Athens, from worship to pampering the gods by supplying them with favorite food and material objects. Paul, in his speech on Mars Hill, introduced the true God who is self-sufficient and doesn't rely on humans to meet His needs. Now, this is the God who truly deserves our worship!

DAY 197

For he satisfieth the longing soul,
and filleth the hungry soul with goodness.
PSALM 107:9

This promise of the Psalms was echoed in Jesus' Sermon on the Mount, when the Lord taught, "Blessed are they which do hunger and thirst after righteousness: for they shall be filled" (Matthew 5:6). Filled with what? Good things like the spiritual fruit of Galatians 5:22–23: love, joy, peace, longsuffering, gentleness, goodness, faith, meekness, and temperance.

DAY 198

— BIBLE READING: —

1 CHRONICLES 23–25; ACTS 18:24–19:10; PSALM 107:10–16

*Then they cried unto the Lord in their trouble,
and he saved them out of their distresses.
He brought them out of darkness and the shadow
of death, and brake their bands in sunder.*
PSALM 107:13–14

Pride sometimes keeps us from asking for help. Deep down we know we just can't get through tough times on our own, but we try anyway. . .and ultimately fail. God didn't create us to be self-sufficient loners. He created us for relationship—most importantly, a relationship with Him. Reach out to Him with your troubled heart and pour out your burdens to Him (Matthew 11:28). He'll lift you out of the darkness and into the light.

DAY 199

Then they cry unto the LORD in their trouble, and he bringeth them out of their distresses. He maketh the storm a calm, so that the waves thereof are still.
PSALM 107:28–29

Storms of troubles come in every life—from physical illness and relationship issues to financial woes and persecution. God promises to hear us when His children call out to Him. He sees the big picture, sometimes quieting the storm and sometimes helping us grow in the situation. Either way, He offers inner peace.

DAY 200

And thou, Solomon my son, know thou the God of thy father; and serve him with a perfect heart and with a willing mind: for the LORD searcheth all hearts, and understandeth all the imaginations of the thoughts: if thou seek him, he will be found of thee.

1 CHRONICLES 28:9

Because He is so different from us, God is mysterious. How can we possibly understand an eternal, all-powerful, all-knowing Being? And yet, God has promised that when we seek Him with all our heart, we'll find Him (Jeremiah 29:13). . .and not only find Him, but *know* Him (Jeremiah 24:7). God is never far away—He's as close as your next thought.

DAY 201

Yet setteth he the poor on high from affliction, and maketh him families like a flock. . . . Whoso is wise, and will observe these things, even they shall understand the lovingkindness of the LORD.
PSALM 107:41, 43

God usually hears from us when we're in crisis mode. We've tried everything else and turn to Him as a last resort. Yet His heart is filled with compassion for His children, and time after time, He responds to our cries for help with answers that are more satisfying than we could imagine. As Jeremiah writes, "It is of the LORD's mercies that we are not consumed, because his compassions fail not. They are new every morning: great is thy faithfulness" (Lamentations 3:22–23).

DAY 202

BIBLE READING:

2 CHRONICLES 4:1–6:11; ACTS 20:17–38; PSALM 108

Through God we shall do valiantly:
for he it is that shall tread down our enemies.
PSALM 108:13

Want to change the world? Partner up with God, and see what amazing things you can do together. With God at your side—guiding you, loving you, blessing you—there's no limit to what you can accomplish (Mark 9:23). Step out in faith, and ask God to work through you. Then wait and see what happens next. Enjoy the ride!

DAY 203

O Lord God of Israel, there is no God like
thee in the heaven, nor in the earth;
which keepest covenant.
2 Chronicles 6:14

Here's a promise applicable to every other Bible promise: God keeps His promises! Human promises fail, deals fall through, people will let you down, but God's promises come with an eternal warranty. Invest in Him for guaranteed returns.

DAY 204

——— BIBLE READING: ———

2 CHRONICLES 7:11–9:28; ACTS 21:15–32; PSALM 109:21–31

For he shall stand at the right hand of the poor,
to save him from those that condemn his soul.
PSALM 109:31

Think about that—God wants to save you from those who question your motives, your sincerity, even your worth as a person. And He stands by your side to defend you! God is, of course, above everything. But in Jesus Christ, He became like us and understands the temptations, fears, and weaknesses we face. Then He sent His Holy Spirit to live in our hearts. God couldn't get any closer to us than that.

DAY 205

And now why tarriest thou? arise,
and be baptized, and wash away thy sins,
calling on the name of the Lord.
ACTS 22:16

"Wash away thy sins. . . ." Sounds too easy and too good to be true, doesn't it? Yet God promises He'll erase all our misdeeds if only we call on Him. God doesn't ask us to become perfect, sinless beings to be saved. He doesn't require any heroic acts or amazing feats. All we need to do is believe His promise. It doesn't get any simpler than that!

DAY 206

The Lord is with you, while ye be with him;
and if ye seek him, he will be found of you.
2 Chronicles 15:2

Words that represent immovable objects often are used to describe God: Rock, Cornerstone, Foundation. He was, and is, and always will be. This is important to remember when it feels like our heavenly Father is far away. The fact is, He hasn't moved. We have. Get back into prayer and into His will—look for Him and He won't hide from you.

DAY 207

*And they came to the chief priests and elders,
and said, We have bound ourselves
under a great curse, that we will eat
nothing until we have slain Paul.*
ACTS 23:14

What ever happened to the forty-plus Jews who promised to fast until they had killed the apostle Paul? Since their plot failed, they may have been a very hungry bunch. Did any of them take their promise so seriously that they starved to death? When we make promises—to God, to ourselves, to our family and friends—how seriously do we take them?

DAY 208

Take heed what ye do: for ye judge not for man,
but for the LORD, who is with you in the judgment.
2 CHRONICLES 19:6

From time to time, we have to make some pretty heavy decisions based on right and wrong. Whether it's at the office, at home, or at church, it isn't always easy to make the right decisions—especially when people try to influence our way of thinking. God promises to be there with us as we make those hard choices. He will give us the guidance we need to make them wise ones (Proverbs 4:7).

DAY 209

O LORD God of our fathers, art not thou God in heaven? and rulest not thou over all the kingdoms of the heathen? and in thine hand is there not power and might, so that none is able to withstand thee?
2 CHRONICLES 20:6

Isn't it interesting how often we, as Christians, lose sight of the fact that we already know we're on the winning side? The fact is, nothing and no one—not even Satan himself—is strong enough to stand against Yahweh. His power and strength are matchless, and His love and concern for His children is limitless.

DAY 210

*Delivering thee from the people, and from the
Gentiles, unto whom now I send thee.*
ACTS 26:17

As long as God has a job for you, you're indestructible.
Jesus promised Paul that the great apostle would
be safe from both Jews and non-Jews (in other
words, *everyone*) while he traveled around preaching
the Gospel. When Paul's job was done, he looked
forward to being with Jesus in heaven, which is "far
better" (Philippians 1:23). There's never a reason
for worry—in Christ, you can't lose!

DAY 211

BIBLE READING:

2 CHRONICLES 24:1–25:16; ACTS 27:1–20; PSALM 115:1–10

Not unto us, O Lord, not unto us,
but unto thy name give glory,
for thy mercy, and for thy truth's sake.
PSALM 115:1

The Bible is filled with tributes to God's holy name. His name is holy and reverent (Psalm 111:9), an everlasting name (Isaiah 63:12), and a name above all other names (Philippians 2:9–10). Yet on any given day, we hear God's name used in ways that are less than worshipful. Today, let's praise—really praise—His wonderful name and thank Him for all His glorious promises.

DAY 212

—— BIBLE READING: ——

2 CHRONICLES 25:17–27:9; ACTS 27:21–28:6;
PSALM 115:11–18

He will bless them that fear the Lord,
both small and great.
Psalm 115:13

Powerhouse CEO. Dedicated office manager. Elementary schoolteacher. Stay-at-home mom. Whatever your profession—and no matter how the world may view it—the Lord considers you an equal to everyone else when it comes to serving Him. He'll reward you in the same manner as all others who revere Him. Nowhere else can you get fair treatment like that!

DAY 213

—— BIBLE READING: ——

2 CHRONICLES 28:1–29:19; ACTS 28:7–31; PSALM 116:1–5

*I love the LORD, because he hath heard my
voice and my supplications. Because he
hath inclined his ear unto me, therefore
will I call upon him as long as I live.*
PSALM 116:1–2

"He hath inclined his ear unto me." No matter how trivial, the Lord promises to listen to your prayers. He wants you to draw near to Him—to talk with Him about everything on your heart (James 4:8). He won't put you on hold. He won't ask you to come back at a later time. He won't tune you out. It's a promise you can count on!

DAY 214

*To all that be in Rome, beloved of God,
called to be saints.*
ROMANS 1:7

Have you ever had a special article of clothing or favorite type of food that is reserved for special occasions? We like to set apart certain parts of our lives to keep them fresh, special, different. God does the same thing with His children. When we accept His gift of grace, we are set apart and hold a special place in the Father's heart.

DAY 215

The truth of the Lord endureth for ever.
PSALM 117:2

All good things, it is said, must come to an end. But that's really not true. This Bible promise assures us that God's Word will last forever. In a world of rapid change and disposable everything, it's comforting to know that our faith is built on the firm, never-changing foundation of "the truth of the Lord." It is permanently recorded in heaven, never to change (Psalm 119:89).

DAY 216

There is no respect of persons with God.
ROMANS 2:11

Rich or poor. Confident or unsure. Man or woman. Joyful or unhappy. Beautiful or plain. The world will judge your worth based on those things and more. But God loves you. . .and He loves you just as much as the next person. Nothing you can say or do could make Him love you any less. His arms are open to you now. Call out to Him and bask in the warmth and comfort of His unconditional love.

DAY 217

— BIBLE READING: —

2 CHRONICLES 34:8–35:19; ROMANS 3:1–26; PSALM 118:19–23

Let God be true, but every man a liar;
as it is written, That thou mightest be
justified in thy sayings, and mightest
overcome when thou art judged.
ROMANS 3:4

When one person causes another pain or disappointment, it's easy to question the goodness of God. Why would He let someone cause such heartache? In a world so full of deceit, how can God be truly pure and blameless? The truth is that God's morality doesn't depend on human morality. As lying and evil festers on earth, God does not, and will not, ever change.

DAY 218

BIBLE READING:

2 CHRONICLES 35:20–36:23; ROMANS 3:27–4:25; PSALM 118:24–29

Thou art my God, and I will praise thee:
thou art my God, I will exalt thee.
PSALM 118:28

The psalm writer promised to thank God—an activity that definitely belongs in our lives today. The apostle Paul couldn't be much clearer about that: "In every thing give thanks: for this is the will of God in Christ Jesus concerning you" (1 Thessalonians 5:18). Now that you know the expectation, will you follow through?

DAY 219

BIBLE READING:
EZRA 1–3; ROMANS 5; PSALM 119:1–8

*That as sin hath reigned unto death, even so
might grace reign through righteousness unto
eternal life by Jesus Christ our Lord.*
ROMANS 5:21

God's power and love covers all sin—from those little white lies to our deepest, darkest, most shameful sins. We don't ever have to fear the punishment of sin, which is death, because He sent His Son to die for us so that we could have eternal life in heaven with Him (John 3:16). Believe in Him. Accept His forgiveness. And look forward to your eternal home.

DAY 220

BIBLE READING:
EZRA 4–5; ROMANS 6:1–7:6; PSALM 119:9–16

Knowing this, that our old man is crucified with him, that the body of sin might be destroyed, that henceforth we should not serve sin.
ROMANS 6:6

Imagine working for a boss named Sin. Along with being demanding and enslaving, Sin keeps its employees chained to an existence that ultimately leads to death. God promises freedom from Sin's dead-end job—freedom through Christ's blood that sets God's "employees," His children, on the fast track of success: eternal life in heaven.

DAY 221

BIBLE READING:

EZRA 6:1–7:26; ROMANS 7:7–25; PSALM 119:17–32

I thank God through Jesus Christ our Lord.
So then with the mind I myself serve the law of God.
ROMANS 7:25

Do bad thoughts, attitudes, or habits get you down? You're in good company. Even the apostle Paul—missionary, miracle worker, Bible author—struggled to do the right things. But Paul ended his true confession with this exciting promise: "With the mind I myself serve the law of God." Never doubt that God, "which hath begun a good work in you will perform it until the day of Jesus Christ" (Philippians 1:6).

DAY 222

Teach me, O LORD, the way of thy statutes;
and I shall keep it unto the end.
PSALM 119:33

There's an implied "if" in this promise: "O Lord, *if* you teach me Your Law, I'll obey it." Is the psalm writer being presumptuous? Not really. God is ready and willing to teach us His truth—and, as we learn more and more of His ways, we should be more and more inclined to obey them. As verse 11 of Psalm 119 says, "Thy word have I hid in mine heart, that I might not sin against thee."

DAY 223

*For I am persuaded, that neither death, nor life,
nor angels, nor principalities, nor powers,
nor things present, nor things to come,
nor height, nor depth, nor any other creature,
shall be able to separate us from the love
of God, which is in Christ Jesus our Lord.*
ROMANS 8:38–39

When things go wrong in life, we may feel as though we've been abandoned by God. But we can find strength and comfort in today's scripture, for God has promised that His love is more powerful than anything in the world—stronger even than death! Our Lord will never keep His love from us, no matter what circumstances life may bring our way. There's no other love like that.

DAY 224

*The law of thy mouth is better unto me
than thousands of gold and silver.*
PSALM 119:72

Nearly every American owns or has access to a copy of the Holy Bible—many even have two or three copies of varying versions. Because of this, twenty-first-century Christians must be careful to not take the Bible for granted. God's words, instruction, wisdom, and encouragement are worth far more than the retail price assigned to the bar code on the cover.

DAY 225

———— BIBLE READING: ————

NEHEMIAH 3:17–5:13; ROMANS 9:19–33; PSALM 119:73–80

I know, O LORD, that thy judgments are right,
and that thou in faithfulness hast afflicted me.
PSALM 119:75

We don't like the idea of punishment. But God knows it helps us grow to maturity—so He's faithful to provide the discipline we need. "We have had fathers of our flesh which corrected us, and we gave them reverence," the book of Hebrews says. "Shall we not much rather be in subjection unto the Father of spirits, and live?" (12:9). The hard things of life may well be God's promised discipline for our good.

DAY 226

—— BIBLE READING: ——

NEHEMIAH 5:14-7:73; ROMANS 10:1-13; PSALM 119:81-88

*For whosoever shall call upon
the name of the Lord shall be saved.*
ROMANS 10:13

The punishment for sin is death. And we're all sinners (Romans 3:23), so does that leave us without hope? God's Word says that all we need to do is believe, and we'll be saved from death. He loves us so much that He sent His only Son to redeem us (1 John 4:9; John 3:16). He has cleared us from all blame and debt—He has freed us from the bonds of sin. He has provided us with the only true source of hope in this world—His Son. Thank Him today for this amazing gift.

DAY 227

NEHEMIAH 8:1–9:5; ROMANS 10:14–11:24; PSALM 119:89–104

So then faith cometh by hearing,
and hearing by the word of God.
ROMANS 10:17

Preaching of the Good News doesn't always come from behind a pulpit. Faith can be born out of the influence of a friend witnessing to another, a Sunday school teacher, a youth sponsor, a mentor, a coach. God promises to plant those seeds of faith in receptive hearts. Our job is to seek out preaching opportunities.

DAY 228

*[Thou] hast performed thy words;
for thou art righteous.*
NEHEMIAH 9:8

Many times throughout the Bible, we see reminders of God's faithfulness. When He promises, He delivers. In this passage, the Jewish leader Nehemiah is reminding the people of God's promises and how He lived up to His Word. That's a good exercise for us today—regularly reviewing God's faithfulness in our lives will give us hope and confidence for whatever circumstances we may face.

DAY 229

Let every soul be subject unto the higher
powers. For there is no power but of God:
the powers that be are ordained of God.
ROMANS 13:1

While we vote our government leaders into office,
God's Word says that "the powers that be are ordained
of God." So while we may fret and question why some
officials are in office, we must turn our concerns over
to God. He has plans that we may not understand. . .
but we may find comfort in the knowledge that the
power held by the leaders of our country has been
given by Him. Say a prayer for our leaders today.

DAY 230

──── BIBLE READING: ────

NEHEMIAH 12:27–13:31; ROMANS 13:8–14:12; PSALM 119:129–136

*Love worketh no ill to his neighbour:
therefore love is the fulfilling of the law.*
ROMANS 13:10

The Bible tells us that love covers many sins (1 Peter 4:8). Here, Paul takes that idea a step further by saying that if we start out by loving others, we won't fall into sins of killing, stealing, lying, and coveting. True Christian love means sincerely caring for others. Such love leaves no room for sins that could hurt another person.

DAY 231

— BIBLE READING: —

ESTHER 1:1–2:18; ROMANS 14:13–15:13; PSALM 119:137–152

For he that in these things serveth Christ is acceptable to God, and approved of men.
ROMANS 14:18

God is pleased with us when we show love to others. When we put the needs and interests of others first, when we go out of our way to help the weak, when we seek peace among our fellow Christians—God has promised that He'll be happy with us. And when God is happy with us, how could we be unhappy?

DAY 232

ESTHER 2:19–5:14; ROMANS 15:14–21; PSALM 119:153–168

*Thy word is true from the beginning:
and every one of thy righteous
judgments endureth for ever.*
PSALM 119:160

Nothing lasts forever. . .except God's Word. Jesus Himself said, "Heaven and earth shall pass away, but my words shall not pass away" (Matthew 24:35). That's because every word of the Bible was penned by men who were inspired by God (2 Timothy 3:16). When you think about this, daily devotions take on a whole new meaning. Yes, God's promises last forever!

DAY 233

My tongue shall speak of thy word: for all thy commandments are righteousness.
PSALM 119:172

Our world is a topsy-turvy roller-coaster ride when it comes to right and wrong, good and bad. Our coworkers, our friends, and our children are bombarded with mixed messages about morality. We can hold fast to the truth of God's Word when we need guidance for life. He'll steer us in the right direction. And we can have an impact on the world by "singing" praises about the blessings He's poured out on us.

DAY 234

*And the God of peace shall bruise
Satan under your feet shortly.*
ROMANS 16:20

Satan's day is coming. It's just a matter of time. While God's children live in a fallen world and deal with the temptations that Satan orchestrates every day, it's sometimes hard not to feel discouraged. Although the final God versus Satan showdown is still to come, God promises His children small day-to-day victories over Satan—with His help.

DAY 235

BIBLE READING:

JOB 1–3; 1 CORINTHIANS 1:1–25; PSALM 123

Who shall also confirm you unto the end,
that ye may be blameless in the day
of our Lord Jesus Christ.
1 CORINTHIANS 1:8

One of the most encouraging promises of the Bible is this: God Himself gives us the strength to live the Christian life. Sure, we're responsible for making the right choices and doing the right thing, but it's God who gives us both the desire and the power to do so. When God started a good work in your life, He intended to see it through (see Philippians 1:6).

DAY 236

But God hath chosen the foolish things of the world to confound the wise; and God hath chosen the weak things of the world to confound the things which are mighty; and base things of the world, and things which are despised, hath God chosen, yea, and things which are not, to bring to nought things that are.
1 Corinthians 1:27–28

The world often labels Christians as weak and fanatical rather than powerful and down to earth. But because the Lord stands opposed to the world and everything it upholds (1 John 2:15–16), we can remain confident that God is behind us as we hold fast to our faith and to the promise that He will strengthen us and protect us from Satan (2 Thessalonians 3:3).

DAY 237

*Know ye not that ye are the temple of God,
and that the Spirit of God dwelleth in you? . . .
For the temple of God is holy, which temple ye are.*
1 CORINTHIANS 3:16–17

Holiness isn't something to be earned or achieved. A Christian can never be good enough, pure enough, or devout enough to somehow earn holiness. God's Spirit lives inside believers. God also says that His house is holy, so we as Christians, through none of our own doing, are holy.

DAY 238

——— BIBLE READING: ———
JOB 10–13; 1 CORINTHIANS 4:1–13; PSALM 128–129

Blessed is every one that feareth the Lord;
that walketh in his ways.
PSALM 128:1

Everyone wants to be happy, and here is God's prescription for joy: honor Him with fear, and walk in His ways. When we do what God tells us to do, happiness follows. Not necessarily wealth, or pleasure, or ease, but the deep-seated contentment that the apostle Paul described in Philippians 4:11. That's a promise worth noting!

DAY 239

──── BIBLE READING: ────

JOB 14–16; 1 CORINTHIANS 4:14–5:13; PSALM 130

But there is forgiveness with thee,
that thou mayest be feared.
PSALM 130:4

Forgiving others is a challenge, isn't it? Sometimes the hurt runs so deep, we just can't seem to let go. But we can find a great example to follow when it comes to forgiving others: the Lord forgets our mistakes as quickly as we can ask His forgiveness (Isaiah 43:25). He even promises to remove our sins "as far as the east is from the west" (Psalm 103:12). Ask the Lord to touch your heart and allow the spirit of forgiveness to envelop your soul today.

DAY 240

What? know ye not that your body is the temple of the Holy Ghost which is in you, which ye have of God, and ye are not your own? For ye are bought with a price: therefore glorify God in your body, and in your spirit, which are God's.
1 CORINTHIANS 6:19–20

God laid down the entire payment—the life of His only Son—to pay for the freedom of every man, woman, boy, and girl who ever has, and ever will, live on earth. In any normal transaction, this purchase would be complete. But God knew the relationship He desires with humans wouldn't be real love unless we willingly accept the gift He offers. Only when we surrender ourselves to God is the transaction complete.

DAY 241

*For I would that all men were even as I myself.
But every man hath his proper gift of God,
one after this manner, and another after that.*
1 CORINTHIANS 7:7

In this passage, the apostle Paul praises singleness. People who aren't married, he says, can devote more of their time and energy to God's service. But Paul also realized that many—likely *most*—people would prefer to wed. And he acknowledged that people have different "gifts." God has promised to "gift" every believer with certain abilities and skills, then to judge them only according to their own—and nobody else's—gifts (1 Corinthians 12).

DAY 242

He bindeth up the waters in his thick clouds; and the cloud is not rent under them. He holdeth back the face of his throne, and spreadeth his cloud upon it. He hath compassed the waters with bounds, until the day and night come to an end.
JOB 26:8–10

When Job uttered these words, he had lost his entire family, all his property, and his health. But instead of raising his fist to heaven in anger, Job *praised* God! Like Job, when things get rough, we can look to God's creation to see evidence of His presence. We can remember God's promise to Noah that those things we take for granted will always be (Genesis 8:22).

DAY 243

But to us there is but one God, the Father, of whom are all things, and we in him; and one Lord Jesus Christ, by whom are all things, and we by him.
1 CORINTHIANS 8:6

Think about all the things you love—your family, your job, chocolate-chip-cookie-dough ice cream, sunrises—and remember where all these things came from. God, our Father, gives us "all things." These "things" are blessings from Him. So the next time you bite into that delicious ice-cream cone, give thanks. He'd love to hear from you.

DAY 244

——— BIBLE READING: ———

JOB 31–33; 1 CORINTHIANS 9:1–18; PSALM 136:1–9

To him that made great lights: for his mercy endureth for ever: the sun to rule by day: for his mercy endureth for ever: the moon and stars to rule by night: for his mercy endureth for ever.
Psalm 136:7–9

Try to list all your blessings, and you'll probably soon realize you can't keep a running tally. There are too many to number! God created all things with only the best for us in mind. Like the moon and the stars, our "nightlights" in the darkness, which He made especially for us to enjoy. Everything He created stems from His loving-kindness, which has no end.

DAY 245

*There hath no temptation taken you but such as is
common to man: but God is faithful, who will not
suffer you to be tempted above that ye are able;
but will with the temptation also make a way
to escape, that ye may be able to bear it.*
1 Corinthians 10:13

Just like the tantalizing scent of warm chocolate-chip
cookies baking, sin's temptations tickle our senses
and desires every day, sometimes several times a day.
Paul reminds us that when it feels like there's no way
to avoid sin, God is faithful to keep temptations at a
level we can deal with. What's more, He promises a
way out of the situation—we just have to keep our
eyes open to His will.

DAY 246

*Ye cannot drink the cup of the Lord, and the
cup of devils: ye cannot be partakers of the
Lord's table, and of the table of devils.*
1 CORINTHIANS 10:21

Never try to convince yourself that "a little sin" is
acceptable. While the apostle Paul was making a
theological argument about food sacrificed to idols,
this "promise" sounds much like Jesus' warning that
"no man can serve two masters: for either he will
hate the one, and love the other; or else he will hold
to the one, and despise the other" (Matthew 6:24).
Don't have a divided mind. Live for God—and God
alone.

DAY 247

I know that thou canst do every thing, and that no thought can be withholden from thee.
JOB 42:2

Whatever God's plan, no one and nothing can stop Him. He can do absolutely anything—even the seemingly impossible. His wisdom and power rise above everything in this world. Remember this promise for your own life, because God has a plan just for you—a plan for your future—and nothing can get in the way of it (Jeremiah 29:11).

DAY 248

——— BIBLE READING: ———

ECCLESIASTES 1:1–3:15; 1 CORINTHIANS 12:1–26; PSALM 139:1–6

For our comely parts have no need: but God hath tempered the body together, having given more abundant honour to that part which lacked. That there should be no schism in the body; but that the members should have the same care one for another.
1 CORINTHIANS 12:24–25

God yearns for unity in His Church. One way unity happens is when a church member is dependent on another. This is why He grants His children their own unique gifts, and why He promises care to the people who need it most. When we work inside God's will, the Church is the living embodiment of God's kingdom on earth.

DAY 249

—— BIBLE READING: ——

ECCLESIASTES 3:16–6:12; 1 CORINTHIANS 12:27–13:13; PSALM 139:7–18

All go unto one place; all are of the dust,
and all turn to dust again.
ECCLESIASTES 3:20

On its face, this "promise" seems a bit dreary: we're all going to die. But a little perspective can turn the negative into a positive. We're returning to dust because that's what we're made of—by God Himself (Genesis 2:7). He knows we're only dust (Psalm 103:14), yet he's able to form us into things of real worth, just like a potter molding clay (Isaiah 64:8).

DAY 250

In the day of prosperity be joyful, but in the day of adversity consider: God also hath set the one over against the other.
ECCLESIASTES 7:14

It's easy to think that when all is well, God is on our side. He's blessing us. He's seeing to all our needs, and we're happy. But when trouble comes, we often feel as though God has left us alone to fend for ourselves. What's harder to see is that God sometimes allows us to go through the rough spots only to bring us to a better place in our lives, and in our relationship with Him. In the tough times, He hasn't abandoned us; He's helping us to grow.

DAY 251

Fear God, and keep his commandments: for this is the whole duty of man. For God shall bring every work into judgment, with every secret thing, whether it be good, or whether it be evil.
ECCLESIASTES 12:13–14

Judges who preside over earthly courts aren't perfect. Only God can be the perfect Judge, who knows all, sees all, and exists everywhere. His judgment promise spans more than just condemning the guilty—He will evaluate every act, even the good, and reward or punish accordingly.

DAY 252

SONG OF SOLOMON 1–4; 1 CORINTHIANS 15:12–34; PSALM 140:9–13

For as in Adam all die,
even so in Christ shall all be made alive.
1 CORINTHIANS 15:22

If you've accepted Jesus as your Savior, this verse promises you an exciting future. You're in line for an "everlasting life" (John 3:16), and there won't be any "death, neither sorrow, nor crying, neither shall there be any more pain" (Revelation 21:4). You'll live with God Himself (Revelation 21:3), enjoying eternity as His beloved child (Revelation 21:7). Wow. . .do you have goose bumps?

DAY 253

But thanks be to God, which giveth us the victory through our Lord Jesus Christ.
1 CORINTHIANS 15:57

When John the Baptist saw Jesus approaching, he remarked, "Behold the Lamb of God, which taketh away the sin of the world" (John 1:29). A few years later, Jesus literally overcame sin and death when He hung on the cross for the sins of humanity. Take hold of the power of Jesus today; ask Him to guide your steps.

DAY 254

BIBLE READING:
ISAIAH 1–2; 1 CORINTHIANS 16; PSALM 142

*Come now, and let us reason together, saith the
LORD: though your sins be as scarlet, they shall
be as white as snow; though they be red
like crimson, they shall be as wool.*
ISAIAH 1:18

You know how hard it is to remove a stubborn stain.
You spot-treat it. You scrub it. You retreat and rewash
it, only to give up in the end. Our sins are like those
hard-to-remove stains. But even though God says
our sins are bright red, they can be made "as white
as snow. . .as wool." He promises to wash our sin
stains—to remove them permanently the first time
around. No rewashing needed!

DAY 255

——— BIBLE READING: ———
ISAIAH 3–5; 2 CORINTHIANS 1:1–11; PSALM 143:1–6

And whether we be afflicted, it is for your consolation and salvation, which is effectual in the enduring of the same sufferings which we also suffer: or whether we be comforted, it is for your consolation and salvation.
2 CORINTHIANS 1:6

It's no secret that Paul went through his share of trouble during his ministry. From imprisonment and persecution to a shipwreck and a mysterious physical handicap (2 Corinthians 12:7), this great missionary of the Christian faith endured years of difficulty to spread the Gospel. But throughout his darkest of days, God provided strength—the same strength offered to Christians to endure troubles in order to share the love of Christ.

DAY 256

*For all the promises of God in [Jesus] are yea,
and in him Amen, unto the glory of God by us.*
2 CORINTHIANS 1:20

Prophecies in essence are promises, and God said throughout the Old Testament that He would send a Savior for all people. In familiar passages like Genesis 3, Isaiah 9, and Micah 5, God hinted or clearly stated that He would provide a way of salvation for sinful humanity. And in Jesus Christ, all those promises were fulfilled!

DAY 257

To whom ye forgive any thing, I forgive also: for if I forgave any thing, to whom I forgave it, for your sakes forgave I it in the person of Christ.
2 CORINTHIANS 2:10

Past hurts have their way of getting stuck in "repeat mode" in our minds, which makes it more difficult to forgive the people who have hurt us. While forgiving others isn't always easy, God calls us to forgive just as He forgives us (Colossians 3:13). He loves us enough to overlook our shortcomings; all He asks is that we do the same for others (Mark 11:25). Praise God today for His amazing love, and ask Him to help you pass that love on.

DAY 258

*And the spirit of the Lord shall rest upon him, the
spirit of wisdom and understanding, the spirit of
counsel and might, the spirit of knowledge
and of the fear of the Lord.*
ISAIAH 11:2

As Jesus developed from a boy into a man, He grew
strong in mind and body and in favor with God
and men (Luke 2:52). Generations before He made
His earthly appearance, God knew exactly how Jesus
would be on earth. Is it any surprise that God has
known us—our personalities, our strengths, our
character flaws—since the beginning of time?

DAY 259

For I will rise up against them, saith the LORD of hosts, and cut off from Babylon the name, and remnant, and son, and nephew, saith the LORD.
ISAIAH 14:22

Babylon was once one of the greatest cities of the world—until God made good on this promise against it. The fulfillment of Isaiah's prophecy against Babylon proved God's absolute power over the kings and peoples of earth, just as He says in Psalm 22:28: "For the kingdom is the LORD's: and he is the governor among the nations." Whatever you read in the news today, remember this: God is in control.

DAY 260

*For we know that if our earthly house of this
tabernacle were dissolved, we have a building
of God, an house not made with hands,
eternal in the heavens.*
2 Corinthians 5:1

Just like old houses that need repair, our bodies
wear out over time. Our joints ache. Our bodies are
destroyed by injury and illness. And although our
earthly bodies will eventually shut down completely,
we can rejoice in the promise of a new body—a
heavenly body created just for us. . .one that will
last for eternity. The aches and pains of this world
are only temporary. That's God's promise to us!

DAY 261

Wherefore come out from among them, and be ye separate, saith the Lord, and touch not the unclean thing; and I will receive you. And will be a Father unto you, and ye shall be my sons and daughters, saith the Lord Almighty.
2 CORINTHIANS 6:17–18

God asks His children to flee from sin not because He's a killjoy or a stick-in-the-mud. The truth is, God wants to receive every person into His embrace, but because of His goodness and His perfection, He cannot embrace someone who harbors sin in his or her heart. Purity—with the help of Christ's cleansing blood—earns God's Fatherhood.

DAY 262

*He hath also stablished them for ever and ever:
he hath made a decree which shall not pass.*
PSALM 148:6

You can count on God's Word. The eternal God has spoken an eternal Law—and we can know the "rules of the game." There will be no surprises, in this life or the next, because God's Word won't change or disappear. In a world that changes so quickly, it's nice to know we have something solid to grasp—the very Word of God Himself.

DAY 263

*Therefore thus saith the Lord GOD, Behold, I lay
in Zion for a foundation a stone, a tried stone,
a precious corner stone, a sure foundation:
he that believeth shall not make haste.*
ISAIAH 28:16

The prophet Isaiah was writing about Jesus Christ,
hundreds of years before His arrival on earth. Jesus
used the same imagery when He called Himself "the
stone which the builders rejected" (Luke 20:17).
Jesus is not only the Foundation of His Church—He
can be the Cornerstone of our lives, if we let Him.
Don't be afraid of building your life on Him.

DAY 264

And God is able to make all grace abound toward
you; that ye, always having all sufficiency in
all things, may abound to every good work.
2 CORINTHIANS 9:8

Do you always feel like you never have quite enough?
After barely covering bills and basic necessities,
how could God expect you to give anything away?
Yet, if you turn control of your needs over to God,
He promises to meet your needs—and then some.
Step out in faith, and prepare to be amazed at the
abundance He has in store for you.

DAY 265

—— BIBLE READING: ——
ISAIAH 31–33; 2 CORINTHIANS 10; PROVERBS 1:10–22

*But he that glorieth, let him glory in the
Lord. For not he that commendeth himself is
approved, but whom the Lord commendeth.*
2 CORINTHIANS 10:17–18

To the world, self-confidence and self-assurance are
vital characteristics to possess. Self-esteem separates
the successful from the unsuccessful and the beautiful
from the ugly. But God sees a person's worth in a
different light. *"Find your self-worth in what I have
done to change you,"* God says. *"The grace extended
through the blood shed by My Son is what guarantees
your importance in My kingdom."*

DAY 266

Therefore it is no great thing if [Satan's] ministers also be transformed as the ministers of righteousness; whose end shall be according to their works.
2 CORINTHIANS 11:15

Are you angered when people use the name of Jesus to lead others astray? Those the apostle Paul calls "false apostles" have done much harm, since the very beginning of the Christian church. But selfish and wicked people—serving the devil himself—will not ultimately win. God has promised to right all wrongs in the end (Matthew 25:41).

DAY 267

And he said unto me, My grace is sufficient for thee: for my strength is made perfect in weakness.
2 CORINTHIANS 12:9

Life would be better if only I had. . . More money. A bigger house. A nicer car. A new career. Sound familiar? But God promises us that our lives can be joyful and complete without all these earthly things (Matthew 6:19–21)—if we only draw near to Him. He is *really* all we'll ever need.

DAY 268

——— BIBLE READING: ———

ISAIAH 39–40; 2 CORINTHIANS 12:11–13:14;
PROVERBS 2:1–15

*He giveth power to the faint; and to them that
have no might he increaseth strength.*
Isaiah 40:29

Every elementary school playground has its token
bully—the kid who likes to pick on children smaller
than him just because he can. God offers strength
and power to the kids getting bullied—and the poor
and weak of the world—to withstand the bullying
of Satan. He won't leave the weak unarmed.

DAY 269

BIBLE READING:

ISAIAH 41–42; GALATIANS 1; PROVERBS 2:16–22

Behold my servant, whom I uphold;
mine elect, in whom my soul delighteth;
I have put my spirit upon him.
ISAIAH 42:1

Hundreds of years after this prophecy was written, it was fulfilled at the baptism of Jesus. At the Jordan River, the Holy Spirit descended on Jesus like a dove—and a voice from heaven boomed, "This is my beloved Son, in whom I am well pleased" (Matthew 3:17). Amazingly, we can experience much the same thing: in salvation, we too receive God's Spirit (Acts 2:38). And we become His much-loved children (Galatians 3:26).

DAY 270

Fear not: for I have redeemed thee, I have called thee by thy name; thou art mine.
Isaiah 43:1

In this life, people will desert and disappoint us. But there is One who promises never to abandon us in our time of need. Our Creator, who calls us by name and claims us as His own, will shelter and strengthen us. He'll walk closely by our side, if we only ask Him to. Call out to Him now; He's waiting to hear from you.

DAY 271

Happy is the man that findeth wisdom, and the man that getteth understanding. For the merchandise of it is better than the merchandise of silver, and the gain thereof than fine gold.
PROVERBS 3:13–14

Proverbs says the Lord built the earth by wisdom and the heavens by understanding (Proverbs 3:19). As Christians, we're called to strive for such wisdom—heavenly wisdom. God promises that getting His understanding is better than silver and gold.

DAY 272

*The wise shall inherit glory:
but shame shall be the promotion of fools.*
PROVERBS 3:35

Notice the word *shall* in this promise. It means something is *going* to happen, though it doesn't say when. In our backward world, fools are often honored while the wise are sometimes shamed. But God will ultimately correct that injustice. In the meantime, be wise (see James 3:17).

DAY 273

ISAIAH 49:14–51:23; GALATIANS 4:1–11; PROVERBS 4:1–19

*And because ye are sons, God hath sent
forth the Spirit of his Son into your
hearts, crying, Abba, Father.*
GALATIANS 4:6

Sometimes when young children clamor for a
parent's attention, they're really just making sure
that their mother or father is there. When we have
the Holy Spirit inside us, the desire to connect with
our heavenly Father becomes as intense as that of a
child with its earthly parents. God longs to hear from
you. . .and He longs to show He cares (1 Peter 5:7).

DAY 274

Keep thy heart with all diligence;
for out of it are the issues of life.
PROVERBS 4:23

What's important in your life? Your career? Your car?
Your house? Your family and friends? God promises
that the most important things life has to offer will
be yours if you keep your heart pure and focused on
Him. Ask Him to help you keep your focus today, and
anticipate the good things He will shower upon you.

DAY 275

—— BIBLE READING: ——
ISAIAH 55–57; GALATIANS 5; PROVERBS 5:1–14

So shall my word be that goeth forth out of my mouth: it shall not return unto me void, but it shall accomplish that which I please, and it shall prosper in the thing whereto I sent it.
ISAIAH 55:11

God's Word is described in Hebrews 4:12 as being sharper than a sword that cuts both ways. John 1:1 also tells us that the Word (Christ) existed from the very beginning. The Word was with God. The Father made good on His promise. Jesus left heaven to come to earth to endure shame, ridicule, and death. He carried out God's plan for salvation.

DAY 276

*Behold, the Lord's hand is not shortened,
that it cannot save; neither his ear
heavy, that it cannot hear.*
ISAIAH 59:1

God is always capable of helping us. His hand is powerful and can save. His ears are open to our cries. But sin in our lives can create barriers between us and God (Isaiah 59:2). Even a man's lack of respect toward his wife will cause prayers to be "hindered" (1 Peter 3:7). God has promised that He can help. Let's not negate that offer by our own sin.

DAY 277

According as he hath chosen us in him before the foundation of the world, that we should be holy and without blame before him in love.
EPHESIANS 1:4

Do you think you're pretty special? Well, you are! You are so special that you were handpicked by God—even before He created the world. Pretty amazing stuff, huh? His love for us is so great that nothing in this world can separate us from Him—not now, not ever. Thank God for this one-of-a-kind love that you can't find anywhere but through Him.

DAY 278

For by grace are ye saved through faith;
and that not of yourselves: it is the gift of God.
EPHESIANS 2:8

We're programmed at a young age that in order to gain something, we have to earn it—that the only way to accomplish anything is by blood, sweat, tears, and hard work. Salvation isn't like that. God tells us simply that His grace isn't earned by our good works, deeds, or behavior. Salvation is a gift to people who put their faith in Him.

DAY 279

BIBLE READING:

ISAIAH 65:17–66:24; EPHESIANS 3:1–4:16; PROVERBS 6:20–26

*For, behold, I create new heavens and
a new earth: and the former shall not be
remembered, nor come into mind.*
ISAIAH 65:17

Life can be good. But it can also be hard. At times,
"hard" outweighs "good." But a time is coming when
God will put all our pain and sorrow behind us, never
to be recalled. Even the earth and heavens we know
will be changed for the better—completely new and
perfect. Since God basically repeated this promise in
Revelation 21, it's definitely worth remembering. . .
especially on those hard days.

DAY 280

And that ye put on the new man, which after God is created in righteousness and true holiness.
EPHESIANS 4:24

Become a "new man," not "sort of a different person." Be "Godlike," not "sort of Godlike." We need to put away the old us as we live for Christ and become new through Him (2 Corinthians 5:17). We can't just change a little; He requires that we change wholly and completely for Him. Only then can we have the amazing life He has promised us.

DAY 281

— BIBLE READING: —
JEREMIAH 3:1–4:22; EPHESIANS 5; PROVERBS 7:1–5

*For this cause shall a man leave his father
and mother, and shall be joined unto his
wife, and they two shall be one flesh.*
EPHESIANS 5:31

God's desire for unity among Christians begins at
home. When a man and woman become husband
and wife, His wedding present is creating one out
of two. Think of it as the reverse of what He did in
the Garden of Eden—instead of creating two distinct
beings (Adam and Eve), He makes them one.

DAY 282

Knowing that whatsoever good thing any man doeth, the same shall he receive of the Lord, whether he be bond or free.
EPHESIANS 6:8

Overworked and underpaid? Not appreciated by your family or friends? Wondering if it's really worth it to do the right thing? This promise provides the encouragement to keep plugging on. Whether anybody else notices or cares about your good work, God does. And His rewards are always the best, anyway.

DAY 283

For to me to live is Christ, and to die is gain.
PHILIPPIANS 1:21

To write these words, the apostle Paul had to embrace the promise of John 3:16: "For God so loved the world, that he gave his only begotten Son, that whosoever believeth in him should not perish, but have everlasting life." This doesn't mean we shouldn't live life to the fullest. Rather, we should not fear death because we are confident of God's precious promise.

DAY 284

*I love them that love me; and those
that seek me early shall find me.*
PROVERBS 8:17

God isn't some elusive being who is always just beyond our reach. He loves us enough that He's made Himself available 24-7. There's never a time—day or night—that we can't reach Him. We have the comfort of knowing that we never have to be alone now or in the future—guaranteed!

DAY 285

JEREMIAH 9:17–11:17; PHILIPPIANS 2:19–30; PROVERBS 8:22–36

He hath made the earth by his power; he hath established the world by his wisdom, and hath stretched out the heavens by his discretion. When he uttereth his voice, there is a multitude of waters in the heavens, and he causeth the vapours to ascend from the ends of the earth; he maketh lightnings with rain, and bringeth forth the wind out of his treasures.
JEREMIAH 10:12–13

The nature of God is almost impossible to describe. As loving and as merciful as He is, the Creator of the universe is just as powerful. As long as we're on His side, we can take comfort in the knowledge that His wrathful power is reserved to defeat Satan.

DAY 286

*Who shall change our vile body, that it may be
fashioned like unto his glorious body, according to
the working whereby he is able even to
subdue all things unto himself.*

PHILIPPIANS 3:21

"The perfect body." In our society, these words
indicate an idealized (and unrealistic) Hollywood
image. In the Bible, it means we'll someday be like
the resurrected Jesus. God has promised to change
our earthly bodies to be like Christ's—bodies that will
never die again. We'll live forever with Him, without
all the aches, pains, and weariness we experience
now. Aren't you eager to enjoy that sleek new model?

DAY 287

BIBLE READING:

JEREMIAH 14–15; PHILIPPIANS 4; PROVERBS 9:7–18

I can do all things through Christ
which strengtheneth me.
PHILIPPIANS 4:13

Rely on God to get you through the tough times. . . because you certainly can't handle everything on your own. Without Christ, we're weak and powerless; with Christ, we're strong and mighty. Ask God today to infuse you with the courage you need to overcome the obstacles you're facing in life.

DAY 288

Blessed is the man that trusteth in the LORD, and whose hope the LORD is. For he shall be as a tree planted by the waters, and that spreadeth out her roots by the river, and shall not see when heat cometh, but her leaf shall be green; and shall not be careful in the year of drought, neither shall cease from yielding fruit.
JEREMIAH 17:7–8

God promises to be a source of life to men and women who trust in Him. God doesn't promise that His water will keep Christians from difficulties—the heat of drought will come—but He does promise that the source of life, hope, and strength will always be there to sustain His children.

DAY 289

— BIBLE READING: —
JEREMIAH 18:1–20:6; COLOSSIANS 1:24–2:15; PROVERBS 10:6–14

And ye are complete in [Christ],
which is the head of all principality and power.
COLOSSIANS 2:10

"Self-fulfillment" is a popular idea, and people pursue it through money, power, and the pleasures of life. But only in Jesus are we truly complete. The One who created the universe and keeps it running (Colossians 1:15–20) will actually live in us (John 15:4). This is a promise of ultimate fulfillment. What more could you possibly hope for?

DAY 290

The labour of the righteous tendeth to life:
the fruit of the wicked to sin.
PROVERBS 10:16

A life without God is a life that will surely end in death (Romans 6:23). However, God promises that if we place our faith and trust in Him—and if we live a life in right relationship with Him—we will receive life. And not just a longer life, but an *eternal* life in heaven, free from all the sadness and problems of the world.

DAY 291

And above all these things put on charity,
which is the bond of perfectness.
COLOSSIANS 3:14

Throughout history, revolutionaries tried to change their circumstances by manipulation, force, and violence. Jesus' take on revolution isn't violent. It isn't hurtful, and it isn't selfish. It's love. He promises unity in love and—even better—He promises that good will be made perfect.

DAY 292

——— BIBLE READING: ———

JEREMIAH 24–25; COLOSSIANS 4:2-18; PROVERBS 11:1-11

Riches profit not in the day of wrath:
but righteousness delivereth from death.
PROVERBS 11:4

No amount of money can protect you from sin and its punishment. That's the bad news. The good news is this promise: "Righteousness delivereth from death." Even better news is that being right with God doesn't cost us a thing—it's "the gift of God" given by Jesus (Romans 6:23). Are you working or worrying for your salvation today? Don't—just accept and enjoy it.

DAY 293

JEREMIAH 26–27; 1 THESSALONIANS 1:1–2:8; PROVERBS 11:12–21

Knowing, brethren beloved, your election of God.
1 THESSALONIANS 1:4

If you panicked every time teams were chosen in phys ed, knowing for sure that you would be picked last, this promise of God is immensely reassuring. Jesus said, "Ye have not chosen me, but I have chosen you, and ordained you, that ye should go and bring forth fruit" (John 15:16). All Christians have the privilege and responsibility to share the Good News. We were chosen to love each other (John 15:17).

DAY 294

BIBLE READING:
JEREMIAH 28–29; 1 THESSALONIANS 2:9–3:13; PROVERBS 11:22–26

The liberal soul shall be made fat: and he that watereth shall be watered also himself.
PROVERBS 11:25

Admit it. You sometimes hesitate to give, because you're skeptical about what you'll get in return. But God's Word promises a huge return on your investment: give a lot and receive a lot; help someone and you'll be helped. Be a cheerful giver (2 Corinthians 9:7) and see what happens. God promises you'll be blessed!

DAY 295

─── BIBLE READING: ───

JEREMIAH 30:1–31:22; 1 THESSALONIANS 4:1–5:11; PROVERBS 11:27–31

And that ye study to be quiet, and to do your own business, and to work with your own hands, as we commanded you; that ye may walk honestly toward them that are without, and that ye may have lack of nothing.
1 THESSALONIANS 4:11–12

God asks His children to be good workers—not lazy, not prone to procrastination. How does this apply to our Christian witness? As Christ's ambassadors, every aspect of our lives—including the forty-plus hours we spend in our careers each week—should reflect a spirit of ability and assurance. When non-Christians see Christians who are capable coworkers, it may open new opportunities for witnessing.

DAY 296

BIBLE READING:

JEREMIAH 31:23–32:35; 1 THESSALONIANS 5:12–28; PROVERBS 12:1–14

Behold, the days come, saith the LORD, that I will make a new covenant with the house of Israel, and with the house of Judah.
JEREMIAH 31:31

God made a promise through the prophet Jeremiah that was fulfilled in Jesus Christ: a "new covenant" that took the place of the Old Testament laws and sacrifices. Jesus' death and resurrection broke the power of the law (Romans 8:2–4) and offered us a new life of spiritual freedom. Aren't you glad?

DAY 297

*Call unto me, and I will answer thee,
and show thee great and mighty
things, which thou knowest not.*
JEREMIAH 33:3

The Lord says if we call out to Him, He "will answer" us. Not He "might answer." Not He "won't answer." But He *will*! When you talk to God, open your heart. You can rest assured that He's listening and that He will offer up the appropriate response in His perfect timing. You can count on it.

DAY 298

BIBLE READING:

JEREMIAH 34:8–36:10; 2 THESSALONIANS 3; PROVERBS 12:21–28

Lying lips are abomination to the LORD:
but they that deal truly are his delight.
PROVERBS 12:22

Parents often refer to their children as their "pride and joy." God loves His children with even more fervent devotion than earthly parents. When we choose to speak the truth—no matter the cost and circumstance—God calls us His joy. It's a daily struggle and decision to choose the path of truth, but one that will be rewarded now and in eternity.

DAY 299

—— BIBLE READING: ——
JEREMIAH 36:11–38:13; 1 TIMOTHY 1:1–17;
PROVERBS 13:1–4

*This is a faithful saying, and worthy of all
acceptation, that Christ Jesus came into the
world to save sinners; of whom I am chief.*
1 TIMOTHY 1:15

The apostle Paul spoke for every Bible writer when
he proclaimed the truth of his message. In a second
letter to Timothy, Paul said, "All scripture is given
by inspiration of God" (2 Timothy 3:16). "For the
prophecy came not in old time by the will of man,"
the apostle Peter added, "but holy men of God spake
as they were moved by the Holy Ghost" (2 Peter
1:21). You can trust *all* the Bible's promises—because
every one comes from God Himself.

DAY 300

— BIBLE READING: —
JEREMIAH 38:14–40:6; 1 TIMOTHY 1:18–3:13; PROVERBS 13:5–13

The light of the righteous rejoiceth:
but the lamp of the wicked shall be put out.
PROVERBS 13:9

Live a life for God in the world today, and others are sure to take notice. You'll stand out—whether it's at work, in school, on the bus, or wherever you go. People will see that you're different when you don't go along with the crowd—you'll be "full of light." Go on! Let your light shine today (Matthew 5:14).

DAY 301

JEREMIAH 40:7–42:22; 1 TIMOTHY 3:14–4:10; PROVERBS 13:14–21

For bodily exercise profiteth little: but godliness is profitable unto all things, having promise of the life that now is, and of that which is to come.
1 TIMOTHY 4:8

Millions of dollars and hours of effort are spent on diet and exercise programs every year. Leading a healthy lifestyle is important, but the truth is that the body is a temporary shell for the Spirit. God urges His children to spend time growing in our faith as well. Unlike diet and exercise, Godlike living has an eternal guarantee.

DAY 302

Take heed unto thyself, and unto the doctrine;
continue in them: for in doing this thou shalt
both save thyself, and them that hear thee.
1 TIMOTHY 4:16

This promise was given by one church leader to another—but the principle applies to all of us. Other people notice when we as Christians believe the Bible and live our lives accordingly. And those who "hear" us—the folks who see our consistent Christian conduct and take it to heart—can be saved by calling on the Jesus we know and serve. And isn't that really what this life is all about?

DAY 303

JEREMIAH 45–47; 1 TIMOTHY 5:17–6:21; PROVERBS 14:1–6

But godliness with contentment is great gain.
1 TIMOTHY 6:6

When new "toys" are advertised on television, it's natural to crave them. We can take a tip from the apostle Paul, who knew what it was like to have it all—or nothing (Philippians 4:12). Greater happiness, he writes, is found by being happy with what you have than by spending money on things that take away from time with your heavenly Father (1 Timothy 6:8–10).

DAY 304

*For God hath not given us the spirit of fear;
but of power, and of love, and of a sound mind.*
2 TIMOTHY 1:7

Toss your fears aside. That's what God wants you to do. Fear doesn't come from Him—so we must embrace the power, the love, and the wisdom with which He has blessed us. Ask God today to remove the fear from your spirit, so you can fully experience the joy-filled life that's possible through Him.

DAY 305

JEREMIAH 49:7–50:16; 2 TIMOTHY 2; PROVERBS 14:23–27

In meekness instructing those that oppose themselves; if God peradventure will give them repentance to the acknowledging of the truth.
2 TIMOTHY 2:25

Ultimately, it's not up to us to change the hearts of those who don't believe the way we do. God promises that if we go about witnessing in a gentle way, He is the One who can soften hard hearts. No need to be discouraged if it seems we just aren't able to reach others; God can work behind the scenes in ways we can't. So keep on reaching out to others with the Good News. . .and leave the rest up to God.

DAY 306

----- BIBLE READING: -----

JEREMIAH 50:17-51:14; 2 TIMOTHY 3;
PROVERBS 14:28-35

All scripture is given by inspiration of God, and is profitable for doctrine, for reproof, for correction, for instruction in righteousness: that the man of God may be perfect, thoroughly furnished unto all good works.
2 TIMOTHY 3:16-17

Have you ever read a book that was so deeply satisfying that it felt as though it was speaking directly to you? The Bible can do just that. God's Word is just as real and relevant today as it was two thousand years ago. For Christians, God's Word promises to supply everything they need to work well for Him. Think of it as a letter penned by God and delivered straight to you.

DAY 307

— BIBLE READING: —

JEREMIAH 51:15–64; 2 TIMOTHY 4; PROVERBS 15:1–9

A soft answer turneth away wrath:
but grievous words stir up anger.
PROVERBS 15:1

Some of the Bible's promises, like those regarding heaven, have a long-term payoff. But others, like Proverbs 15:1, have a practical, everyday benefit. Since God created people, He knows what they're like—and He knows that angry words generate additional anger. Gentle answers are like water on a fire, cooling the heat and limiting the damage. Can you put this promise into practice today?

DAY 308

*Paul, a servant of God, and an apostle of Jesus
Christ, according to the faith of God's elect, and the
acknowledging of the truth which is after godliness;
in hope of eternal life, which God, that cannot
lie, promised before the world began.*
TITUS 1:1–2

You've heard lots of people say, "I'm telling the truth."
But the truth mentioned in today's scripture reading
is the only truth that has eternal impact. This "truth"
refers to God's sacrifice of His only Son for our sins
(John 3:16). God promises that if we believe and
accept His gift, we will have eternal life. Put your
trust in God's Word today.

DAY 309

─── **BIBLE READING:** ───

LAMENTATIONS 2:1–3:38; TITUS 1:10–2:15; PROVERBS 15:18–26

It is of the Lord's mercies that we are not consumed, because his compassions fail not. They are new every morning: great is thy faithfulness.
LAMENTATIONS 3:22–23

Consider the renewal you get from the cleansing water when you bathe. After a workout, or a tough day at work, or a hot summer day, nothing feels better than a relaxing shower. God's love and grace renew with a cleansing power greater than any shower. He faithfully provides renewing streams to His children every morning of every day.

DAY 310

The LORD is far from the wicked:
but he heareth the prayer of the righteous.
PROVERBS 15:29

God promises to listen to us when we're "righteous." The other side of the coin is that sin in our lives breaks the fellowship we could enjoy with God. There are any number of ways to mess up—Peter once wrote that a man's prayers can be hindered if he just shows disrespect to his wife (1 Peter 3:7)— but consciously maintaining a close relationship with God brings countless benefits.

DAY 311

—— BIBLE READING: ——
EZEKIEL 1:1–3:21; PHILEMON; PROVERBS 16:1–9

*A man's heart deviseth his way:
but the Lord directeth his steps.*
PROVERBS 16:9

God has given us free will. We have the ability to make choices for our own lives—whether good or bad. So how can we be sure we're making the right choices? Ask God. His Word gives guidance and direction for each step we take (Proverbs 3:6). He will always lead us on the right path—guaranteed (Psalm 37:23).

DAY 312

EZEKIEL 3:22–5:17; HEBREWS 1:1–2:4; PROVERBS 16:10–21

*The wise in heart shall be called prudent:
and the sweetness of the lips increaseth learning.*
PROVERBS 16:21

Have you ever been so enraged by injustice or blatant sin that all you wanted to do was shout and throw things? Your reaction may be a prodding of the Holy Spirit who is saying, "Hey, wait a second. God is not happy about this!" But it's in our reaction that God can be found. Confronting others in a calm and gentle way may allow them to see the truth, and you will honor God at the same time.

DAY 313

Yet will I leave a remnant, that ye may have some that shall escape the sword among the nations, when ye shall be scattered through the countries.
EZEKIEL 6:8

Judgment day had come for the idol-worshipping people of Israel. Through the prophet Ezekiel, God promised to punish His chosen people for their disobedience—but to stay true to His earlier promises to Abraham and David, God also promised to save some of the people. How? By scattering them among the other nations. Look around today—Jewish people the world over confirm God's complete truthfulness.

DAY 314

EZEKIEL 8–10; HEBREWS 3:1–4:3; PROVERBS 17:1–5

Better is a dry morsel, and quietness therewith,
than an house full of sacrifices with strife.
PROVERBS 17:1

"Anger management" has spawned an entire industry, with books to read and courses to take, all "guaranteed" to help control one's temper. How comforting it is to read these ancient words about our God: "But thou art a God ready to pardon, gracious and merciful, slow to anger, and of great kindness" (Nehemiah 9:17). To enter into God's presence is to come into a place of "peace and quiet."

DAY 315

Neither is there any creature that is not manifest in his sight: but all things are naked and opened unto the eyes of him with whom we have to do.
HEBREWS 4:13

We can hide our hearts from our spouses. We can hide our hearts from our friends. We can hide our hearts from our coworkers. But no matter how hard we try, we can't hide our hearts from God. He sees and knows everything about us—what we think, what we feel, what we do. And yet He still loves us (Ephesians 2:4–7)!

DAY 316

That ye be not slothful, but followers of them who through faith and patience inherit the promises.
HEBREWS 6:12

Life sometimes makes our Christian faith seem all but impossible. God knows this. He's also given us examples of people who endured in their faith despite extreme circumstances—Noah, Abraham, Moses, Mary, Paul. God asks for faithfulness and guarantees a reward in return: eternal life in heaven.

DAY 317

A foolish son is a grief to his father,
and bitterness to her that bare him.
PROVERBS 17:25

Nobody likes this kind of Bible promise, but it's in God's Word for a reason. When we do wrong, we hurt other people, especially those closest to us. Remember God's promise of sowing and reaping—we get back what we put into life (Galatians 6:7–8). Be wise, and bring joy and blessing to the people you love!

DAY 318

BIBLE READING:

EZEKIEL 16:44–17:24; HEBREWS 8:1–9:10; PROVERBS 18:1–7

For I will be merciful to their unrighteousness,
and their sins and their iniquities
will I remember no more.
HEBREWS 8:12

It's easy to point out someone else's shortcomings, isn't it? But we are called to love and forgive others despite their mistakes (Mark 11:25–26). Follow God's example, as He promises to continue to love us even though we fail Him. And He forgives us every time we ask—never to bring it up again. Ask Him to help you extend forgiveness to someone today.

DAY 319

But if the wicked will turn from all his sins that he hath committed, and keep all my statutes, and do that which is lawful and right, he shall surely live, he shall not die. All his transgressions that he hath committed, they shall not be mentioned unto him: in his righteousness that he hath done he shall live.
Ezekiel 18:21–22

Humans strive for youthfulness through diet, exercise, and cosmetics—all in an effort to delay aging and death. God offers the ultimate antiaging guarantee: eternal life. In heaven there will be no over-the-hill birthday celebrations, no uncertainty about the future, no wrinkles, no hair loss, no death.

DAY 320

EZEKIEL 20; HEBREWS 10:1-25; PROVERBS 18:18-24

*A man's belly shall be satisfied with the fruit
of his mouth; and with the increase of
his lips shall he be filled.*
PROVERBS 18:20

Think about the imagery of this verse for minute:
If bitter, awful words come from your mouth, you'll
feel that bitter awfulness in the pit of your stomach.
If you're speaking sweet, healthy words, that's what
the rest of your system will register. What more do
we need to say about this promise?

DAY 321

EZEKIEL 21-22; HEBREWS 10:26-39; PROVERBS 19:1-8

*For ye have need of patience, that, after ye have
done the will of God, ye might receive the promise.*
HEBREWS 10:36

We often ask God for things, even though we may
not be living according to His will. We continue to
disobey Him; but when we have a need, we selfishly
call on Him and yet wonder why nothing seems to
be going right in our lives. God doesn't guarantee
us a trouble-free life, but He does promise to bless
our lives and fulfill His promise to us if we will obey
His commands (Deuteronomy 5:29, 6:18).

DAY 322

But without faith it is impossible to please him:
for he that cometh to God must believe that
he is, and that he is a rewarder of
them that diligently seek him.
HEBREWS 11:6

Faith pleases God. It's that simple. He's not a holy Santa Claus who simply wants to hear our requests; He wants our trust and belief that He exists and is able to supply our every want and need. When we follow through with our faith and seek Him, He'll bless our lives beyond our wildest dreams.

DAY 323

*He that keepeth the commandment
keepeth his own soul.*
PROVERBS 19:16

Which of God's promises can be bigger than this one? By keeping God's Word—by studying and applying it to our lives—we keep our souls. What does that mean? We preserve and protect them, from the destruction of sin and hell. In Jesus' own statement, "I know that his commandment is life everlasting" (John 12:50).

DAY 324

Wherefore seeing we also are compassed about with so great a cloud of witnesses, let us lay aside every weight, and the sin which doth so easily beset us, and let us run with patience the race that is set before us.
HEBREWS 12:1

For those who wonder if they could run around the block, the many references to running in the Bible can be daunting. Yet, as believers who know that the finish tape ends in heaven, tying on those spiritual sneakers can be an exercise in trusting God's promise of eternal life. Like Paul, one day we can rejoice that "I have fought a good fight, I have finished my course, I have kept the faith" (2 Timothy 4:7).

DAY 325

───── **BIBLE READING:** ─────

EZEKIEL 29–30; HEBREWS 12:14–29; PROVERBS 20:1–18

The just man walketh in his integrity:
his children are blessed after him.
PROVERBS 20:7

Our lifestyles. Our morals. Our values. Our priorities. However we choose to live, we are affecting the lives of our children. We are called to teach our children God's ways and to live our lives so that they may learn Christlike behavior from our actions (Isaiah 54:13). If we obey God and walk closely with Him, He promises that our children will be happy.

DAY 326

BIBLE READING:

EZEKIEL 31–32; HEBREWS 13; PROVERBS 20:19–24

Say not thou, I will recompense evil;
but wait on the LORD, and he shall save thee.
PROVERBS 20:22

We say we want justice, and we want it now. Earthly justice, however, is sometimes a masquerade for revenge. When someone wrongs us somehow, our immediate response is retaliation—an eye-for-eye and tooth-for-tooth mentality. God tells us to have patience when we're wronged. He'll deliver justice that's better than any revenge we can dole out.

DAY 327

Let no man say when he is tempted, I am tempted of God: for God cannot be tempted with evil, neither tempteth he any man.
JAMES 1:13

God is always good. Though He may allow you to experience some tough things, He'll never try to trip you up. Since He can't be tempted to do wrong, He won't tempt you to do wrong either. In fact, He's promised that "God is faithful, who will not suffer you to be tempted above that ye are able; but will with the temptation also make a way to escape, that ye may be able to bear it" (1 Corinthians 10:13).

DAY 328

I will feed my flock, and I will cause them to lie down, saith the Lord GOD. I will seek that which was lost, and bring again that which was driven away, and will bind up that which was broken, and will strengthen that which was sick: but I will destroy the fat and the strong; I will feed them with judgment.
EZEKIEL 34:15–16

God is our Good Shepherd. When we are hungry, He will feed us. When we are tired, He will give us rest. When we lose our way, He will find us again. When we are hurting, He will tend to our wounds. And when we are sick, He will infuse us with His strength. No matter how weak you are in spirit, He will never leave you lost and alone. Reach out to Him and allow Him to envelop you in the shelter of His love.

DAY 329

*And the fruit of righteousness is sown
in peace of them that make peace.*
JAMES 3:18

A farmer will never sow a kernel of corn and reap a thistle bush. When he plants good, quality seeds, he'll have a harvest of good, quality produce. That's similar to what God promises His children who sow peace about them. Peace planted in situations and lives around you will yield righteousness and goodness—crops that glorify the Creator!

DAY 330

*Whoso keepeth his mouth and his tongue
keepeth his soul from troubles.*
PROVERBS 21:23

Here's one of those really practical promises of the
Bible. Watch your mouth—be careful what you
say—and you'll avoid a lot of trouble. Easier said
than done, perhaps. . .but that's where God's Holy
Spirit comes in. Remember the fruit of the Spirit
in Galatians 5:22–23? The last one mentioned is
temperance, or self-control. Control your speech.
Doesn't that sound better than saying something
you'll regret?

DAY 331

— BIBLE READING: —

EZEKIEL 40; JAMES 5:7–20; PROVERBS 21:25–31

The effectual fervent prayer of
a righteous man availeth much.
JAMES 5:16

God promises that our prayers are packed with spiritual "punch" if our lives are right with Him. While He hears *all* prayer, it's comforting to know that we can have a bigger impact if we are living in obedience to Him. Thank God today for the awesome effect we can have with our prayer lives if we are faithful Christians.

DAY 332

Whom having not seen, ye love; in whom,
though now ye see him not, yet believing,
ye rejoice with joy unspeakable and full of glory.
1 PETER 1:8

Only a select group of people ever got to interact with Jesus during His thirty-three years on earth. The good news is that present-day Christians can express the same love that first-century Christians held for the Messiah—all it takes is belief and trust. Our love for Jesus leads to a joy that's so great that words cannot describe it.

DAY 333

BIBLE READING:

EZEKIEL 43:13–44:31; 1 PETER 1:13–2:3; PROVERBS 22:10–23

And if ye call on the Father, who without respect of persons judgeth according to every man's work.
1 PETER 1:17

There's an old saying that goes like this: "The ground is level at the foot of the cross." What it means is that anyone and everyone needs Jesus, and anyone and everyone can come to God through Him. God doesn't care if you're rich or poor, healthy or sick, man or woman or child. He loved everyone enough to send Jesus—and promises to accept all who come through Him.

DAY 334

BIBLE READING:
EZEKIEL 45-46; 1 PETER 2:4-17; PROVERBS 22:24-29

*Be not thou one of them that strike hands,
or of them that are sureties for debts.*
PROVERBS 22:26

The Bible is a very practical book, and this verse tells us not to promise our own lives and goods for other people's debt. In modern terms, that's cosigning a loan—and it can put you in a real bind, according to the next verse: "If thou hast nothing to pay, why should he take away thy bed from under thee?" (Proverbs 22:27). Look to the Bible for guidance on spiritual matters. . .but also for the practical questions of life.

DAY 335

[Jesus,] who his own self bare our sins in his own body on the tree, that we, being dead to sins, should live unto righteousness: by whose stripes ye were healed.
1 PETER 2:24

A strange concept. . .that the wounds of another—Jesus Christ—could actually heal us. But that's what God's Word says. Jesus was wounded and ultimately died for our transgressions (Isaiah 53:5). And through His sacrifice—His promise—we are able to experience an abundant life—and be freed from the punishment of sin forever (Hebrews 9:28).

DAY 336

*For he that will love life, and see good days,
let him refrain his tongue from evil, and his
lips that they speak no guile: Let him eschew evil,
and do good; let him seek peace, and ensue it.*
1 PETER 3:10–11

Want joy? Want a happy life? God promises these things to those who restrain themselves from indulging in gossip and sin. Go after goodness and peace, He commands, and He'll deliver on His promise.

DAY 337

Bring me in before the king, and I will shew unto the king the interpretation.
Daniel 2:24

This was a promise from a condemned man. Daniel and the other "wise men of Babylon" faced a death penalty if they couldn't tell King Nebuchadnezzar what his dream meant. . .after telling him what his dream *was*. But Daniel wasn't desperately trying to buy time. He trusted God, who told him both the king's dream and its interpretation. Though we'll probably never be in such a dramatic situation ourselves, we can still trust God for all the wisdom we need in life.

DAY 338

DANIEL 4; 2 PETER 1; PROVERBS 23:26–35

How great are his signs! and how mighty are his wonders! his kingdom is an everlasting kingdom, and his dominion is from generation to generation.
DANIEL 4:3

No matter who we are or where we come from, God's Word—and His promises—apply to us. Rich or poor, man or woman, beautiful or plain. From ancient history to today, His Word stands timeless. We can count on our Father, our Friend, to keep His promises. We never have to wonder. We never have to question. We never have to worry. All we must do is believe.

DAY 339

My son, eat thou honey, because it is good;
and the honeycomb, which is sweet to thy taste:
So shall the knowledge of wisdom be unto thy
soul: when thou hast found it, then there shall be a
reward, and thy expectation shall not be cut off.
PROVERBS 24:13–14

God's wisdom may be well beyond our grasp, but He still encourages His children to seek for and grow in wisdom. God says His wisdom is as sweet and soothing to the soul as honey is to the taste buds. God guarantees His wisdom can be the nourishment we need to sustain us and give hope for today and tomorrow.

DAY 340

*The Lord is not slack concerning his promise,
as some men count slackness; but is longsuffering
to us-ward, not willing that any should perish,
but that all should come to repentance.*
2 PETER 3:9

What promise is Peter describing? The promised return
of Jesus Christ. Many people question it: "Where is the
promise of his coming? for since the fathers fell asleep,
all things continue as they were from the beginning of
the creation" (2 Peter 3:4). But Peter reminds us that
time is different with God: "Beloved, be not ignorant
of this one thing, that one day is with the Lord as a
thousand years, and a thousand years as one day" (2
Peter 3:8). God will keep His promise. He's just giving
people more time to turn to Him.

DAY 341

DANIEL 7:15–8:27; 1 JOHN 1:1–2:17; PROVERBS 24:28–34

God is light, and in him is no darkness at all.
1 JOHN 1:5

When your life seems overcome by darkness, there is hope. Place God in the center of your life, and He will lift your spirit. He will give you the strength and courage you need to overcome even the most challenging obstacles (Psalm 31:24). Find the faith that you need for life: look to the light.

DAY 342

*And now, little children, abide in him; that,
when he shall appear, we may have confidence,
and not be ashamed before him at his coming.*
1 JOHN 2:28

God didn't create humans to be entirely self-
reliant. He knows that we need Him, even when
we don't realize it ourselves. John reminds us of
our reliance on God by telling us to live with His
help. By relying on Him to help us day to day and
in the difficult times, our relationship with the
Creator is strengthened.

DAY 343

DANIEL 11–12; 1 JOHN 3:1–12; PROVERBS 25:13–17

*Beloved, now are we the sons of God, and it doth
not yet appear what we shall be: but we know
that, when he shall appear, we shall be like
him; for we shall see him as he is.*
1 JOHN 3:2

Most of us have days when we just don't like ourselves
very much. Our appearance, our health, our attitudes,
our temptations—so many issues trouble us. But God
has promised Christians a day when all our problems
will be over. We'll actually be like Jesus—perfect
and complete in every way. "And every man that
hath this hope in him purifieth himself, even as he
is pure" (1 John 3:3).

DAY 344

—— BIBLE READING: ——

HOSEA 1–3; 1 JOHN 3:13–4:16; PROVERBS 25:18–28

It is not good to eat much honey: so for men to search their own glory is not glory.
PROVERBS 25:27

Substitute "chocolate" for "honey," and everyone can understand the first half of this verse. God's promise is that too much of the sweet stuff can make us sick—just like the pursuit of personal recognition can hurt us. Follow the apostle Peter's advice, instead: "Humble yourselves therefore under the mighty hand of God, that he may exalt you in due time" (1 Peter 5:6).

DAY 345

For whatsoever is born of God overcometh the world: and this is the victory that overcometh the world, even our faith.
1 JOHN 5:4

Does sin have control over your life? Do you have daily struggles with temptations so great, you're not sure you can overcome them? God says that, as His children, we have "the victory that overcometh the world." And that power is through our faith (Romans 6:14). Ask God to strengthen your faith today, and thank Him for providing you a way to overcome sin in your life (1 Corinthians 10:13).

DAY 346

He that abideth in the doctrine of Christ,
he hath both the Father and the Son.
2 JOHN 1:9

Jesus' teachings came with a simple message: "If you're in with Me, you're in with My Father." For His disciples, this was a radical thought. Until the time of Christ, the Hebrews considered God a lofty ruler who could only be approached through ritual and tradition. Jesus offers a real relationship to Christians—not only with the Son, but with the Father as well.

DAY 347

Which have borne witness of thy charity before the church: whom if thou bring forward on their journey after a godly sort, thou shalt do well.
3 JOHN 1:6

Hospitality is good for everyone—especially for those doing the hosting. God has promised good to Christians who help out other Christians. And He's promised good to Christians who help out "strangers"—people not already in our circles. As we bless others with our kindness, God is blessed. . . and He blesses us in turn.

DAY 348

*Turn unto the Lord your God: for he is gracious
and merciful, slow to anger, and of great
kindness, and repenteth him of the evil.*
JOEL 2:13

Have you ever found yourself so far out of sync with
God that you felt you could never make things right
with Him again? God's Word says that we can always
return to Him. His love can bridge even the deepest
chasm and bring you back into a close relationship
with Him (Ephesians 2:4–7).

DAY 349

BIBLE READING:

JOEL 2:18–3:21; REVELATION 1:1–2:11;
PROVERBS 27:18–27

*Blessed is he that readeth, and they that hear
the words of this prophecy, and keep those
things which are written therein.*
REVELATION 1:3

Many people avoid the book of Revelation, with its mysterious prophecies and images of destruction. But, right off the bat, it promises happiness to anyone who will read it, hear it read, and obey what it says. With an offer like that, why wouldn't you study Revelation?

DAY 350

Better is the poor that walketh in his uprightness,
than he that is perverse in his ways,
though he be rich.
PROVERBS 28:6

In a world that worships money, this Bible promise
seems crazy. It's better to be poor? Well, yes. . .if
you're walking in honor. Do what's right, every time,
and God will provide the most amazing payback—
perhaps here on this earth, but for sure in heaven
to come.

DAY 351

BIBLE READING:

AMOS 4:6–6:14; REVELATION 3; PROVERBS 28:9–16

*Behold, I stand at the door, and knock: if any man
hear my voice, and open the door, I will come in
to him, and will sup with him, and he with me.*
REVELATION 3:20

God is waiting for you. He's knocking on the door
of your heart right now. Invite Him in. . .and open
your heart to everything He has to offer. Prepare to
be infused with an overabundance of peace and joy
that only He can bring into your life (John 15:11).

DAY 352

He that tilleth his land shall have plenty of bread: but he that followeth after vain persons shall have poverty enough.
PROVERBS 28:19

Hard work reaps rewards. God shows this throughout scripture, and Jesus teaches it in His parables. An honest day's work yields fair pay, and honest transactions are blessed by God. The flip side of this promise is that a lazy person who squanders his time will lose whatever blessings and riches he may acquire. Learn from this promise—now get to work!

DAY 353

*But I will sacrifice unto thee with the voice of
thanksgiving; I will pay that that I have
vowed. Salvation is of the LORD.*
JONAH 2:9

For promises made in strange places, this one wins
the prize: Jonah spoke these words inside a fish's
stomach. A disobedient prophet, trying to run from
God, Jonah had three days and nights in a living
prison cell to consider his spiritual obligations. . .
and this prayer is what resulted. The point for us?
Don't slip so far into disobedience that God uses
extreme measures to get your attention!

DAY 354

*Nation shall not lift up a sword against nation,
neither shall they learn war any more.*
Micah 4:3

One day, after Jesus comes again, a new kingdom will
be established on a new earth (Revelation 21:1). In
this new kingdom, not only will wars cease, but there
will be no crying, no death, and no pain (Revelation
21:4). And that's not just the opinion of some hermit
or cult leader. . .that's a promise from God Himself.

DAY 355

MICAH 4:6–7:20; REVELATION 7:9–8:13; PROVERBS 29:9–14

For the Lamb which is in the midst of the throne shall feed them, and shall lead them unto living fountains of waters: and God shall wipe away all tears from their eyes.
REVELATION 7:17

One day, as we enter eternity with our brothers and sisters in Christ, we will be freed from all sin, sickness, and suffering. Our Good Shepherd, Jesus Christ, will take all earthly woes and remove them from us—permanently. Never again will we shed a tear. Never again will we feel pain. Never again will we experience loss. All we'll know is joy and peace as we praise and worship the Lord for eternity.

DAY 356

NAHUM; REVELATION 9–10; PROVERBS 29:15–23

A man's pride shall bring him low:
but honour shall uphold the humble in spirit.
Proverbs 29:23

For most of us, it's difficult to admit when we're wrong or that we need help. But God asks us to humble ourselves and put pride aside. God guarantees honor to His children who can look at a situation and consider the needs of others before themselves—a direct command of scripture (Philippians 2:3).

DAY 357

*The kingdoms of this world are become the
kingdoms of our Lord, and of his Christ;
and he shall reign for ever and ever.*
REVELATION 11:15

Watch the evening news, and you'll probably become depressed. We live in a troubled world, full of bad people and bad situations. But the day is coming when Jesus will rule with perfect justice. Everything bad will be done away with; life will be ideal. And His reign will last forever. Now that's a promise worth remembering!

DAY 358

ZEPHANIAH; REVELATION 12; PROVERBS 30:1-6

*Every word of God is pure: he is a shield
unto them that put their trust in him.*
PROVERBS 30:5

It's human nature to question whether someone is being truthful. We know from past experiences that some people are unable to be honest and forthright. It's refreshing that there is Someone whom we can believe—at all times—for "every word" of His has been proven. Not once has He been dishonest or indirect (1 Kings 8:56). Place your trust in Him today.

DAY 359

*And I heard a voice from heaven saying unto me,
Write, Blessed are the dead which die in the
Lord from henceforth: Yea, saith the Spirit,
that they may rest from their labours;
and their works do follow them.*
REVELATION 14:13

Some of God's greatest promises are wrapped up in the guarantee of eternal life for His children. He promises no more death, no more sickness, no more tears—but it's not just the absence of bad things that will make heaven so wonderful. Heaven will be a state of pure happiness as we worship the King of kings who humbled Himself to be born to a poor Jewish couple in a barn.

DAY 360

And the LORD shall inherit Judah his portion in the holy land, and shall choose Jerusalem again.
ZECHARIAH 2:12

Modern Jerusalem is a troubled place. Violence, terrorism, and war have plagued the city for generations. But God still loves His ancient capital, and promises that He will make it the center of government in an ideal new world. Next time you hear Jerusalem mentioned in the news, think ahead to an age of perfect peace and prosperity—ruled by Jesus Himself.

DAY 361

ZECHARIAH 5–8; REVELATION 16:4–21; PROVERBS 30:21–28

Behold, I come as a thief. Blessed is he that watcheth, and keepeth his garments.
REVELATION 16:15

Although we know Christ will return one day, it often slips to the backs of our minds as we walk through life. But He wants us to wait in anticipation—to always be ready. For He says He will come "as a thief." There will be no grand announcement, no set date or time for His return. So prepare your heart, and wait expectantly.

DAY 362

BIBLE READING:

ZECHARIAH 9–11; REVELATION 17:1–18:8; PROVERBS 30:29–33

The Lamb shall overcome them: for he is Lord of lords, and King of kings: and they that are with him are called, and chosen, and faithful.
REVELATION 17:14

Satan will be vanquished. Jesus is and will be King of all. Why? Because He was and is and will be. There's no guarantee greater than that. He deserves our honor and praise and gratitude because He thought enough of each of us to offer grace. He calls us His chosen and faithful ones. Hallelujah!

DAY 363

BIBLE READING:

ZECHARIAH 12-14; REVELATION 18:9-24; PROVERBS 31:1-9

There shall be no more utter destruction.
ZECHARIAH 14:11

Ever since Adam and Eve blew it in the Garden of Eden, humanity has lived under a curse. We work hard, get old, and die. We experience disease, accidents, and emotional trials. Life becomes, at times, very hard. But someday, in God's good time, that will all change. The curse will be lifted, and God will make everything new (Revelation 21:5)!

DAY 364

Who can find a virtuous woman?
for her price is far above rubies.
PROVERBS 31:10

A good wife, a faithful husband, a long-lasting marriage
. . .these are all gifts from God. From the moment Eve
was created, God wanted marriage to be a permanent
blessing and a unifying force in an often fragmented
society (Genesis 2:24). God honors marriage (Hebrews
13:4), and He blesses wives and husbands who seek
His will and His promises.

DAY 365

MALACHI 3-4; REVELATION 21-22; PROVERBS 31:18-31

For I am the LORD, I change not.
MALACHI 3:6

Life is full of change. People change. Careers change. Our circumstances change. Our opinions change. In a world where there is no consistency, what a blessing we have in this promise that God has given to us: "I am the LORD, I change not." His Word is guaranteed—now and forever. Amen!

SCRIPTURE INDEX

Revelation

DEVOTIONAL INSPIRATION FOR EVERY MAN!

3-Minute Prayers for Men
This devotional prayer title packs a powerful dose of inspiration into just-right-sized readings for men of all ages and backgrounds. Each of these 180 prayers, written specifically for devotional quiet time, meets you right where you are—and is complemented by a relevant scripture and question for further thought.

Paperback / 978-1-64352-043-8 / $4.99

The 5-Minute Bible Study for Men
In just 5 minutes, you will *Read* (minute 1–2), *Understand* (minute 3), *Apply* (minute 4), and *Pray* (minute 5) God's Word through meaningful, focused Bible study. *The 5-Minute Bible Study for Men* includes more than 90 Bible studies that will speak to your heart in a powerful way.

Paperback / 978-1-64352-274-6 / $5.99